D1203938

SKYLARK PRESS

LUC LEESTEMAKER

The
INTENTIONAL ARTIST

Stories From My Life

ALSO BY LUC LEESTEMAKER

Luc Leestemaker: Paintings

LUC LEESTEMAKER

The
INTENTIONAL
ARTIST

Stories From My Life

SKYLARK PRESS

Copyright © 2010 by Luc Leestemaker

All rights reserved. No part of this publication may be reproduced, distributed, or transmitted in any form or by any means, or stored in a database or retrieval system, without the prior written permission of the copyright owner of this book.

Author's note: Some of the names, locations and details of events in this book have been changed to protect the privacy of persons involved.

Skylark Press
269 S. Beverly Drive, Suite 1188
Beverly Hills, CA 90212
Visit our website at www.skylarkpress.com

For more information about Luc Leestemaker visit:
www.lucleestemaker.com

First Edition, January 2010

Copy Editor: Yvonne Milosevic
Design & Art Direction: Chris Davies
Portrait Photography: Bjoern Kommerell

The author is grateful for permission to use the following copyrighted material:
The Mother's Signature, Dr. Bernhard W. Bail,
The Masters Publishing Company, Beverly Hills.

The essays *Return of the Muse, Time* and *Alchemy* are reprints from earlier publications.

Library of Congress Cataloguing-in-Publication Data

Leestemaker, Luc; The Intentional Artist
Includes bibliographical references and color plates

ISBN: 978-1-4243-2400-2

*To Emily, who continually helps me to understand
the meaning of my journey.*

The unexamined life is not worth living.

— *Socrates*

But to live outside the law, you must be honest.

— *Bob Dylan*

CONTENTS

Acknowledgements

I OWE A LOT of gratitude and thanks to many people who have helped me, consciously or unconsciously, in the journey of my life that has led to this extraordinary moment. I apologize in advance to the many I'm sure I will forget to mention, but here are a few that have marked themselves in my head, people that have, dead or alive, become constant fellow-travelers whom I regularly consult for advice or moral support. Thank you Emily for your never-wavering love and support; to Allen W., for your great insights and humor; to Chris for always coming through, even in stormy weather, for being a great friend and partner, and for your magnificent talents in design and art direction; to Yvonne Milosevic for your wonderful editing skills and your ability to turn English-Dutch into English with my voice intact; to the formidable Roger Ma, the most reliable print agent in the world; and to all who have inspired and supported me over the years: Nick, Larry, Michael, Susan, Alan V. and Philip N., Sallie and Team, Lisa, Lorna, Leah, Kevin and Joni. Thank you Ruysdael and Rembrandt van Rijn, William Turner and John Constable, Picasso and Willem de Kooning, Mark Rothko and Anselm Kiefer, for allowing me to stand on your shoulders and learn from your insights. Thanks to all my collectors who live with and are the guardians of my paintings, and thank you America, my new homeland, for giving a little Dutch boy the chance to make a dream come true…

Luc Leestemaker's Memento Vitae

BY PETER FRANK

THE DUTCH WERE some of the earliest European settlers in North America. Luc Leestemaker followed in their footsteps a few hundred years later, bringing with him a similar sensibility and a few similar reasons for coming. Like his explorer/settler forebears, he's something of a wanderer, an adventurer – a guy who looks out over the limitless horizon and into the big sky and wonders what's out there, what's up there, and what will happen if he goes in search. Whatever it is, it has to provide more psychic elbow room than the small-town ethos that spooked Luc even in Amsterdam. The same intimacy and up-close informality with which the Dutch charm others can get under the skin of certain Dutch folk who would like to scratch their own itch. That is why Luc came here – not to be an artist, but to re-become one; to get out from under the accomplishments of his artistic family and to go wide in his art and his life.

You can take the Hollander out of Holland, but you can't get the Holland out of the Hollander. Luc may be the paint-craziest Dutch-American since Willem de Kooning, and the most ambitious since Colonel Tom Parker.

His purview may be entirely free of the provinces, but some parts of his old land have remained. Luc paints with abandon but makes art with a purpose. Not just to express himself, but to open our eyes. And he tells stories with a wink, but also with a reason. Not just to entertain, but to give a little insight into life and its lessons.

Dutchmen have been imparting moral wisdom to one another, and the rest of us, since they first started pulling their land from the sea. You don't fight off that much water and learn nothing. One thing the Dutch learned is how fleeting – nasty, brutish and short, perhaps – life is, so the fact that we're uniquely sentient, and painfully aware of (if resistant to) our fate, must mean that there is some higher power. One with a wicked sense of humor, no doubt, but with a certain compassion as well. Seafaring people learn that you live by myriad rules, or else – and even then, you die. No surprise, then, that the memento mori, the symbolic reminder of mortality, is a favorite subjective device of Dutch painters, especially those expert in still life. But even the most expansive landscape painters could paint the hand of death into a bosky dell or lowering sky.

There's a finger-wagging aspect to this grumbly fatalism that Luc Leestemaker explicitly rejected when he moved to this eternally and wackily hopeful country. The lessons he's learned about life, especially now that he's settled in for the long haul as an artist and done so comfortably (if not easily), are far more optimistic than his countrymen could possibly believe. But, like them, he wants to share what he's learned and what he's come to believe. As opposed to all the hucksters who roam this ever-credulous land selling people on riches and power and immortality, Luc wants to sell you simply on the delights of living an unanticipated life; of not being afraid to take initiatives or even risks; of savoring both the moments that happen to you and that you make happen. Mistakes, Luc relates, are not simply learning experiences; they're aesthetic experiences, moments of theater in your own life that everyone can understand but no one has had quite like you've had. Whether you earned what happened to you, you now own it, so polish it and put it on the mantel.

The overall lesson Luc has learned and wants to impart to us through his painting and, now, writing, is Carpe Diem – seize the moment. If stuff happens, ride with it; if stuff can happen, make it happen. Calculate the risk, but take it. Take a look at Luc's paintings, how he has transited from his early attempts either to force a shape or color or simply let it occur to a harmonious balance between jumping into the void with a few wild brushstrokes and then building on the best of those brushstrokes until a coherent composition emerges. Maybe that composition, or a reasonable armature thereof, existed in the painter's mind – certainly after two decades of often feverish productivity, Luc has a relationship with his painting that requires no second-guessing – but he still knows that accidents can be not just the impediments to goals, but the breakthroughs in vision, the suddenly found path to new goals, or new ways to the original targets. Or both.

A painting doesn't just happen, but it does happen. As Luc has learned from painting – and from living to paint – don't just expect the unexpected, hope for it, and know that the ride will be wild and your job is to steer it. Creativity, after all, is not the exclusive province of the artist, but can – must – be accessed by everyone seeking not just to exist, but to live; indeed, not just to live, but to triumph. It's a craft to survive, Luc Leestemaker advises us, but an art to thrive.

Peter Frank is Editor of Fabrik Magazine in Los Angeles, senior curator at the Riverside Art Museum, former art critic at the LA Weekly, Angeleno magazine, the Village Voice, and the SoHo Weekly News, organizer of exhibitions around the world and author of numerous art books, monographs and catalogues.

CHAPTER ONE

Rite of Spring

IN OUR FAMILY, it was quite obvious that the Mother was the one in charge. After her came my older brother, whom she must have declared crown prince while still in utero. Both my father and I felt somewhat wary of the eldest; with him you never quite knew what you were up against. He went to fancy schools and had learned to speak Greek and Latin at an early age. This sibling, whom I had secretly nicknamed The General, made all decisions relating to both the purchase and maintenance of things in our household. He immediately nipped in the bud any attempts either by my father, me or my predominantly mute sister to have a say regarding activities in the home.

Perhaps because of his knowledge of foreign languages, the deep understanding of instruction manuals he seemed to possess, or maybe just because he was so good at pretending to know something about everything, my mother steadfastly turned to him for help. A sociological explanation would often accompany simple domestic decisions, such as purchasing a washing machine, toaster or mixer from Krups but, God forbid, not Philips. When the time came to buy a new family car, my brother argued earnestly – and, to my mind, abstrusely – that because Le Corbusier had been a genius of architecture and fought for social change with his experimental buildings in the suburbs of Paris, we should therefore purchase the Citroën DS with hydraulic suspension. This purchase was so outrageously beyond the budget of a lower middle class administrator like my father, both in upkeep and gasoline usage, that the car spent most of its life in the garage.

My father continued his daily journey to work on his old bicycle, and if and when the Citroën saw the light of day, it was usually with my brother behind the wheel and my father sitting next to him, pretending to be in charge. Observing the two of them, I knew this was just for show – not unlike a military regime that installs a puppet president to keep up the pretense of democracy. The real brains behind the operation sat in the backseat, camouflaged as a demure mother figure who carefully orchestrated the workings of the family unit to make sure that The General would forever be her loyal lackey. Looking back at my childhood, it's pretty clear that my parents, like many others, should have never been allowed to fulfill one of the most complex and ingenious biological acts of nature. All I can say is, thank God for the fact that most of their actions were unconscious. Despite the cruelties bestowed upon us children, there was such a lack of awareness on their part that I somehow managed to keep my identity intact and slip through the cracks of their dictatorial regime.

From an early age, I treated the household pretty much like a bed and breakfast run by mentally challenged commoners, with whom I got along just fine – as long as they left me alone. In hindsight, I see that as a result of The General's iron reign as the Mother's viceroy, I chose my own strategy. If he was the perfect, responsible son who excelled at school and cultivated social networks by bringing home friends and their parents, I did exactly the opposite and created my own social systems outside the home, which kept their attempts at control safely at bay. I made friends in the rough neighborhoods down by the railway station, where the middle class barely dared to tread, or spent endless hours in the forest that began at the end of our street. Once, during a birthday party at our home, I let The General know that I was on to his charade of feigning absolute knowledge of all things technical by declaring that my brother could repair anything. A few days later, broken alarm clocks, staplers, irons and radios starting showing up, which caused him to spend many an evening sweating and swearing over his small, wobbly IKEA desk until he had no choice but to admit defeat. My maneuver cost me some physical consequences – he threw me down the stairs a few times – but that was well worth the strategic advance I had made. An actual coup détente... Don't mess with me, for I know your weaknesses...

I remember one event from my childhood that has stayed with me all my life, as it was the first demonstration of the Universe's creative powers that I became conscious of. One evening, as the family sat dourly around the dinner table in their usual impersonation of Van Gogh's The Potato Eaters, things were about to change. I had just learned in school that this day, March 21, was the first day of spring and an occasion worth celebrating. At home, the family didn't seem to know or care about seasons and the joy of renewal. Instead, they were silently working their way through watery potatoes and overcooked vegetables. Desperate to get out of the house, I decided to give magic a chance. I started off by rehashing the teachings I had received that day. I noticed The General eyeing me suspiciously, threatened that I was grabbing the spotlight that was supposed to be his alone. Nevertheless, it seemed that my talk began to have an effect. I kept it going, and said, "And so, in order to celebrate this moment in time, we are now going to get up from the table – leave everything as it is – and we are going to walk to the hallway and put on our coats, and we are going to take a short walk through the forest to celebrate this wondrous day."

I got up from the table and moved slowly toward the door. I sensed a surprised silence behind me, and then, the clattering sounds of cutlery dropping on the table and chairs scraping over the parquet floor. To my astonishment, I next heard the sounds of bodies shuffling behind me. This could be over at any moment, I thought, but just the fact I had gotten them this far was a miracle. I didn't dare look behind me; I felt it would break the hypnotic spell I had somehow managed to cast over them. Speaking with a low, reassuring voice, like one does to put a nervous dog or horse at ease, I continued, "And now we put on our coats and we walk just a little distance into the forest..." I opened the front door. Still no objection voiced from behind me, not even from The General. There we went; me in front, the rest of the family following, with willing bodies and helpless minds. It must have been a peculiar sight – a young boy leading a family single file through the dense forest that felt as much my home as my own bedroom.

I remember coming home that evening feeling powerful and victorious. It's the same feeling when, out of the blue, a check arrives, alleviating some urgent financial pressures; or a painting appears from under my brush that sings and oozes colors full of joy and confidence. That evening I had somehow been able to break through the sluggish walls of cold Calvinist doctrine with the heart and voice of nature itself. For one moment, the forest had brought life and wonder into the home of the dead. Back inside, everyone took off their coats, adjusted themselves, and almost immediately fell back into their comfortable, dull routine. Instead, I walked up to my room and sat down on my bed in wonder, feeling as if I had just discovered magical powers. That evening brought a gift and discovery into my life that has sustained me ever since: the enduring force and undeniable evidence of the existence of the creative heart.

CHAPTER TWO

Breakfast With the Queen

GROWING UP, I had a huge crush on the crown princess, Beatrix. When I heard she had started dating someone—a German prince, no less—I was not pleased at all. In fact, I was outraged. Admittedly, there was a substantial age difference between us, some twenty years, which doesn't count in your favor if you're a ten-year-old boy. If only she would have been patient and waited a few years, I could have been her most loving and devoted husband.

But no one seemed to care about my feelings, and the doomed day of her matrimony soon approached. The only help I received in sabotaging her wedding came in the form of some punks who were disgruntled with the entire royal family. Following an old Dutch tradition, they caused a good number of street disturbances that brought out the water cannons and police in riot gear, while just blocks away the young, seemingly happy couple were seen waving from their carriage as they traveled from city hall to the church. The majority of the country was glued to their TV sets while these ceremonies took place, but I had seen enough. I took my dog out for a long, sulking walk to console myself.

On a grey, drizzling Saturday morning some fifteen years later, my friend Cornelius and I stepped out of a squatted home whose host had treated us generously the entire night with many rounds of his new water pipe, stuffed to the rim with a wide variety of exotic imports. For a few weeks now, we had been working tirelessly on the renovation of an old theater closed down by city officials to make way for a new development. We left the scaffolding and boarded up windows in place and opened up one of the back doors to let ourselves inside. Our idea was to renovate the theater from the inside out, and at night we visited one of the city's unguarded construction sites and loaded our bicycles with as many materials as we could carry.

The official opening ceremony would consist of removing all of the building materials on the outside, throwing open the heavy oak entrance doors and voilà! —the party would begin. Cornelius and I brainstormed ways to make the opening of the squatted theater the biggest success possible. I had already suggested a few weeks earlier that it might be fun to invite the queen for the opening and have her say a few words. My letter and invitation had spoken of Her Majesty, Queen Juliana, as our Big, Reigning Friend, whom the people of Amsterdam would love to welcome as one of their own.

I was not pleased with the lack of response from the palace, especially in light of her daughter's earlier rejection. Princess Beatrix had at this point been married to her German prince for quite some time, and I read regular reports in the papers about his paralyzing depressions that suggested her increased loneliness and isolation came as a result. I couldn't say I felt too sorry or was too surprised.

That particular Saturday morning, we were sizzling with energy and not at all ready to call it a night. We stood on the doorstep for a while, taking in the scene as the rain fell on the black asphalt and the traffic lights turned green-orange-red in their slow, monotonous cycle. I don't know who came up with the idea first, but suddenly we were staring at each other with wide, stupid grins plastered on our faces.

"Breakfast with the queen?" Cornelius asked, incredulous.

"Why not?" I replied, "She hasn't responded to our letter and this would be a good way to invite her personally."

We looked out over the silent, empty street as we mulled over the notion of breaking bread with Her Majesty. "I think it's an excellent idea," Cornelius finally said. "Do you think we need to do some shopping on the way, or will she have breakfast stuff in the house? Or, I guess I should say, palace?"

"We'll whip up something in the kitchen, don't worry," I replied, and we set off toward the car.

It took us about thirty minutes to get to the palace. I'd grown up in the area and knew my way around the grounds. In fact, the queen's dentist lived on our street, and a number of times, we children stood on the sidewalk waving in an instant serenade as her black Cadillac cruised by, the Novocain probably still wearing off in her face. The window would slowly open and an elegant, white gloved hand waved back at us. Magical times. But Princess Beatrix, my long-ago object of adoration, was a different story. It had not been as easy to communicate with her.

Would that all change today, I wondered? Would I gain easier access to the family, and to her, by becoming acquainted with her mother first? We parked the car a bit away on the wide boulevard across from the palace and started walking lazily toward the front gate, each of us probably wondering exactly where and when the bluff would end.

"Excuse me, sir," we asked a bored-looking guard, "We're here to make breakfast for the queen. Could you tell us how to get to the kitchen?" The soldier seemed in no mood for pleasantries and told us in no uncertain terms to get lost.

"He's probably embarrassed that he doesn't know," Cornelius said, as if to excuse him. Not knowing what to do next, we headed for the public park adjacent to the palace grounds. We kept walking for a while, each lost in our own thoughts and working hard to clear our heads of the previous night's haze.

Suddenly, we stopped short. Before us was an opening under the fence, barely larger than the mining activities of a rabbit, but a hole nevertheless. We kicked the ground around a bit with our boots. "This must be the entrance?" I asked Cornelius innocently, hoping he would suggest that we call it a day and turn around. But he didn't.

"Absolutely!" he replied, already trying to wedge his cumbersome body through the opening. With a heavy heaving and squeaking, the old, rusty gate gave enough to let us through. Moments later we found ourselves on the official palace grounds. We started walking again, slowly now, in the way people walk in the black of night—their arms stretched out in front of them—tasting the emptiness and not knowing what to expect next.

For a while the terrain didn't look much different. Then, through a clearing in the trees, we saw a mini golf course adjacent to a tennis court. Further down, a few bicycles strewn carelessly on the lawn. Silent witnesses. We walked on, as on eggshells, and finally we glimpsed the back of the palace. There she stood, in white marble, a Dutch version of the Taj Mahal, rising up in front of us. This building, which had held such magical meaning for me as a child, was now shrinking in stature before my eyes. The omnipotent quality of the immense palace of my childhood had metamorphosed into something almost gaudy, like the faux palazzos erected by the Beverly Hills nouveau riche.

"Look, there, that must be the study." Cornelius' voice sounded muffled as his entire face was pressed against a window. Like a building inspector taking measurements to make sure everything is done per code, he slowly moved sideways. "Oh yes, look here, that's the living room, I bet. A grand piano! I wonder who plays?"

I called out to him when I discovered the kitchen, which had not been that difficult. Palace or not, it was simply a kitchen door. As my hand pushed lightly against the handle, I prayed the door would be locked. But it wasn't. It opened seamlessly, and we stood on the threshold looking inside, expecting and hoping that now, finally, the alarms would start ringing. But the only sound I heard was the buzzing inside my head as the cannabis started to wear off. We couldn't turn back now. We looked at each other with bewilderment and then, almost simultaneously, stepped inside. Cornelius started inspecting the contents of the refrigerator while I rummaged through some cabinets looking for a pan to boil water.

"How do you think she likes her eggs?" I asked my partner in crime, without looking up. Silence. "Cornelius?" I turned around.

Cornelius stared at me helplessly, his hands flopping up in the air like an actor in an amateur television series for children. I started laughing at the ridiculous scene, but then I heard a metallic click and saw the young soldier behind him, a rifle pushed into my friend's back. The rifle was shaking, and looking up at the solider, I noticed that he was shaking, too. I needed to do something. But what?

"Hellooo there," I called out with the friendliest voice I could muster, a voice that must have sounded like a cartoon character. "Do you by any chance know how the queen likes her eggs?"

Cornelius started laughing hysterically and both his and the guard's body were now moving together as if in a waltz, both shaking uncontrollably and still connected to each other by the guard's rifle. The soldier took in the scene in utter disbelief, trying to comprehend what his eyes were registering. Finally, he reached for his walkie talkie and hoarsely whispered some alarm codes into the device. After that, we stood frozen in place; this was not a good time to make any sudden movements. From a distance we heard the sound of tires crunching on the gravel. Four impeccably dressed soldiers rode in from the front lawn on their bicycles, rifles extended in front of them. The captain, or whoever it was, took the lead and started guiding us gently out of the kitchen.

"Do you know how the queen likes her eggs?" I asked him, thinking I might as well keep up the charade.

"Yes, yes, we're going to sort all that out for you," he answered patiently, as if talking to a child—or his demented grandmother. Slowly we made our way over to the front lawn and grand entrance of the palace, the very spot where the world's dignitaries had arrived in limousines and carriages for hundreds of years to be met by the reigning monarch. We passed the same guard we had met on our way in, and he stared back at us in disgust. The security detail then settled us into a holding cell in an improvised police station across the street while they searched our car for bombs and anarchist literature.

After an hour or so we were led out of our cell and sat down in front of a well-worn desk that looked like something from a Goodwill store. A quiet, older man with a kind expression turned to address us. "Gentlemen," he began, "Please tell me why you have woken me up early on a Saturday morning." He sounded friendly, reasonable, like someone you could trust. I decided to stay in character and told him all about our theater in Amsterdam; how hard we had worked to get it all ready in time; how hurt we had been when we received no reply from Her Majesty to our invitation.

This now seems so innocent that it's hard to imagine this conversation in light of all the terrorist attacks worldwide in recent years. But this was all that happened: a totally reasonable conversation with the head of Security Services, who politely educated us about palace protocol. Not only that, he also promised that a new letter, with a copy to him, would be promptly attended to by Her Majesty's secretary.

Our exchange ended with a polite but urgent request not to go out and brag about our morning's adventures, as that would mean security would have to lay a constant cordon of guards around the palace grounds to keep the copycats away. In other words, we must never, ever mention this event again. With that, he sent us on our way, wishing us much luck with the opening of the theater.

I don't remember our journey home. I presume I went straight to bed, exhausted from the experience. I think it was this event more than anything that shaped my ongoing education in deductive analysis and deconstruction; to learn that things often may not be at all what they seem, for good or bad.

After waking up later in the day, groggy from just a few hours of restless sleep, I sat behind my typewriter and composed a new letter for the queen, recounting our quest to visit with her for breakfast in order to get her to come to our opening. As the head of security had promised, within two weeks a letter with the official seal of the royal family arrived. Sadly, Her Majesty would not be able to join us for the opening, but she nevertheless wished us much success with our endeavors.

Some ten years later, disguised in a business suit and coifed hair, I finally met my princess, who by this time had succeeded her mother, at a reception for a cultural festival for which I'd started working. It was a long lineup, with time enough to exchange just a few polite pleasantries. But when it was my turn, and I looked into those eyes I'd longed for since the days of her betrothal to the German prince, I couldn't help but wonder what it would have been like if that guard had not interrupted us in the kitchen... Cornelius and I stumbling up the stairs, looking for the right room, carrying a silver tray with some toast, marmalade and eggs as we fulfilled our mission to deliver breakfast to our Big, Reigning Friend. Would Her Majesty have intervened on my behalf?

I still see Queen Beatrix sometimes on TV, laying wreaths and holding court on her birthday. The passage of time has transformed her into a kind, elderly lady; close-ups reveal sad eyes. She has long ceased to be the object of my desire and has grown into an impersonal symbol, just another head of state. And only in recent years, thinking back to the journey on that grey Saturday morning, have I come to realize that my pilgrimage to the palace was in fact not dedicated to her, or to her mother, but symbolized nothing less than the ongoing conquest of love itself.

CHAPTER THREE

Death of an Encyclopedia Salesman

A LONG TIME AGO, I used to sell encyclopedias. Once a week, I met up with a ragtag team of salesmen gathered in the stately home of the regional manager, who had built his estate from the overrides in commission generated by his sales team. Each seller would open his leather briefcase and out came the loot for the week. Then all eyes turned to me, curiously eyeing the contents of my pseudo attaché—a tattered plastic bag. Five nights a week, this unlikely team of knowledge distributors fanned out over the country to make house calls and convince parents that they needed to invest in their kids' future; that 60-something spinsters addicted to Scrabble and crossword puzzles should reward themselves; or that a leather-bound set would make the living room look really swell.

They called me the dream seller. I had earned this honorary title because week after week I showed up with the largest number of signed order forms. But the one-armed bookkeeper Johannes, who looked like a character straight out of the movie Dr. Strangelove, refused to pay my commission right away and would tell me placidly, "Let's wait till next week." He knew the meaning of my title all too well, and saw, due to a law that allowed buyers to cancel their orders within a cooling off period of 24 hours, a constant stream of cancellations arriving on his desk.

We salespeople collected our checks; drank coffee with a little Dutch gin called jenever on the side; and devoured homemade apple pie baked by the manager's wife. War stories of the past week's adventures of the hunted and captured prey were exchanged. The cozy setup even included a large bucket filled with floral bouquets for each salesman to take home to "the wife." The highlight of each meeting was, undoubtedly, the motivating sermon delivered by our fearless leader. Sometimes, in the middle of his speech, he would suddenly excuse himself; later we found out that he suffered from seizures at irregular intervals. But the attacks would subside as quickly as they came on. With a look of surprise, he would walk back into the room, wipe the corners of his mouth, and continue his discourse.

I had more or less fallen into this unlikely profession, enticed by an acquaintance who convinced me that it was extremely easy money. All it took was a few evening hours of driving through the Dutch countryside making house calls with a trunk full of sample books, thus insuring there would always be one set sized to fit the bookcase in question. Small towns and farming communities seemed especially susceptible to the argument that the available knowledge of a 20-volume encyclopedia would dramatically increase their children's chances in a hostile and competitive world. Admittedly, my passionate performances seduced many customers in the moment, only to have them stricken with buyer's remorse and running for the nearest post office come morning. But plenty of customers happily embraced the new addition to their household and made my work the easiest money ever earned. Meanwhile, I spent my days staring out the window in the grey, provincial industry town where I lived, writing incomprehensible existential plays and prose. When a friend who now lived in San Francisco came to visit and invited me back to the States, it didn't take long to pack my bags and head for the airport.

After a good bit of sightseeing on the West Coast, I wanted to taste some real American life. Scanning the classifieds in a local newspaper, I was pulled in by an ad for a profession I thought I had already mastered; thus, I became the newest member of the Encyclopedia Britannica sales team in Santa Rosa, a sleepy town bordering the wine country in Northern California. As an advance on my first sales commission check, the team manager took me to a local Sears and fitted me in a polyester suit. I received a stack of heavily thumbed inquiry forms and was sent on my way in my second-hand Chevy van, which looked like the preferred means of transport for a serial killer—an old black monster with no windows other than the cracked windshield.

Little did I know I had become part of a long tradition of the immigrant's first rung on the societal ladder. I felt as if I had just entered one of my own existential plays as the lead actor. The inquiries turned out to be so old that, due to the frequent migration of the American population, most of the addresses were no longer valid. In other cases, a husband would open the front door, and, looking for a way to kill some time, would call out to his invisible wife, "Honey, the encyclopedia salesman is here!" Followed by a "What is that accent, son? Come on in!" I spent many afternoons getting the most wonderful introduction into American life. But three months later I had sold exactly one set; the sales commission wasn't even enough to cover the cost of my suit, the price of the sales leads, or the gasoline used to drive up and down the 101 freeway in search of customers.

One evening, I was driving through the deserted town of Bodega Bay on my way back home. With some excitement, I realized that this little town—featured in Alfred Hitchcock's movie The Birds—had given me my first taste of the United States. Well, that, and the back alleys of Los Angeles from the TV series, Starsky & Hutch. I turned up the volume of the oldies jazz station, took a long drag of my cigarette and flipped it out of the window. A few seconds later I noticed a flame shooting up from under the old

Chevy; the cigarette butt had somehow managed to get into the exhaust pipe. I stopped the car with a wild screeching of the brakes and ran for cover. As I lay by the side of the road, hands covering my ears and waiting for a thunderous explosion, it occurred to me that the car had come to a halt in the center of town, which I recognized from one of the movie's pivotal scenes in which Tippi Hedren is seriously assaulted by an army of birds.

A few minutes passed. Nothing was moving; the town was deep asleep. My black monster quietly simmered in the middle of the road, its exhaust still burning like a peaceful torch. After ten minutes I started to feel slightly ridiculous waiting for an explosion that might never occur. I walked up to the Chevy with the careful tread of a burglar—as if not wanting the vehicle to notice my approach—turned off the engine and threw my polyester jacket around the tail pipe. Then I started the old beast up again and sat behind the wheel. For the rest of my journey back to the city, I made sure to put out my cigarettes in the ashtray. I regularly inspected the exhaust through my mirror but the jacket had done its job well. Looking at the passenger lying on the seat next to me in a sad, half-burnt heap, I knew instantly that this would be my final night as a proud representative of Encyclopedia Britannica.

I expected a scolding when I notified the sales manager, but instead he treated me to a hearty lunch in a local diner and complimented me on persevering a lot longer than he and his team had expected. I tried a few other professions after that, including selling sandwiches and carrot cakes to office employees. That worked just fine until a recruiter of the Life Spring Center, a place that organized wellness courses, took an interest in me and tried to convince me I could do a lot better than selling sandwiches. I sat in on a few training sessions during which executives ran around the room pretending to be different types of wild animals to unleash their inner spirit and creativity.

But I was not ready to be 'saved', and, as if to mock them, I left the catering job and hauled dirt at a construction site for a while. A part of me loved the chaotic and gigantic space that this new country offered me, but the bigger part of me felt uncomfortable and strangely claustrophobic with its large open spaces. After a few more weeks I packed my bags and headed home, where I returned to my easy sales gig with the local encyclopedia publisher and listened to the weekly epileptic rants of the regional manager.

Somehow though, my exposure to life in America, with its boundless sky in total contrast to Holland's permanent low-hanging fog, had rattled me out of my lackadaisical cocoon. I started treating life with more zest and professionalism; the Life Spring instructor would have been proud. Choice and intention became part of my life. I soon traded a dreary existence without perspective for a career in creative marketing, which eventually culminated in my own consulting company in Amsterdam. It would take me eleven years to realize that my first short visit to the United States had been a reconnaissance flight, and the fear of large, open space that is the hallmark of this country would, over time, come to have an irresistible pull. When the second opportunity of a lifetime arrived, I had built up enough courage to voluntarily abandon my successful career. As a result, I sold the return part of my airline ticket within a few days after setting foot again on American soil.

CHAPTER FOUR

Thoreau's Dream

PERHAPS AS A result of living in the U.S. for almost half my life, I have developed a strong preference for everything clean, sparkling and new. I love new homes that have freshly conquered nature; I love clean, new clothes; I love that "new car" scent, even though my car is no longer exactly new. There was a time, though, when old things held the most charm for me. In my youth I spent many Saturdays hanging around a public dumpster. With a practiced eye, I studied everyone who discarded their castoffs from garage sales and attic purgings. A sense of adventure always accompanied these outings; amidst the rubble of old furniture, broken glasswork, and heaps of old magazines and books, I knew I just might find some sort of treasure. I have decorated entire apartments with furniture abandoned by others. As for my wardrobe, I regularly frequented a store in Amsterdam called Vintage USA, which sold woolen suits from the fifties – including the narrow ties. You could only wear them a few times before the aged fabric burst at the seams, so I returned to the store on a monthly basis to replenish my stack of old suits. Around that time I found some old spectacles in our attic that had belonged to my grandfather, the painter, and several of his waistcoats and jackets. I treated each piece like gold and started incorporating them into my daily attire.

I found something very inviting and melancholy about the past, which may have had to do with the no-nonsense climate of the 1950s into which I was born. Perhaps the material and stylistic frugality of those days was a reaction to the Second World War. If you look at furniture of that period, most everything is boxed, hard, meticulous and merciless. No comfortable chairs to sit in. No time for dreams or fantasies. This was a time to invest in safety and security; double locks became the norm on the front and back doors of all homes, especially in the lower middle class street that I grew up on. It's no wonder that a budding artist in that environment is destined to develop wanderlust—one starts traveling as soon as possible to cultures that have not done a garage sale of their history and kept intact some of the connections and references to dreams of other times.

In my early twenties, under the strong influence of authors like Leo Tolstoy and Herman Hesse, I had my own Back to Nature fantasies. One day, while aimlessly riding my bike several miles outside the grey industrial town I lived in, I found what would come to double as my own "Walden Pond," though at that time I had not yet heard of Emerson or Thoreau. An old disheveled farmhouse leaned along a winding country road, looking as if one strong wind might topple it to the ground. I fell in love with the place the moment I saw it.

After a few inquiries in the area, I soon located the owner—a retired farmer who had built himself a brand-new abode made of concrete that seemed to have as little to do with farming as possible. Witnessing my desperately romantic babbling about the decrepit homestead, and perhaps fearing my temporary insanity would soon disperse, he immediately sat me down to sign a contract. A day later I returned with a deposit, picked up the keys, and the place was mine. Almost immediately upon entering the dank, crumbling structure, my romantic ideas vanished and apprehension set in. What was I actually going to do with this place? I walked aimlessly from room to room, trying to conjure images of a warm home full of life. I was going to have to find a lot of used furniture to fill this place.

Suddenly, I received quite a shock when a grotesque figure appeared at the window, its face pressed flat against the glass. After a moment, I recognized the visage as the farmer who had told me where to find the owner, and who, apparently, was now my neighbor. "Name's Hendrik; just checking in with you city folk," he said unapologetically when I opened the front door. He studied me from head to toe. "So, you're gonna play farmer?" The fact that his tone was not condescending but actually friendly almost seemed like even more of an insult. Can these farmers smell when city people start having dreams of the country? I think he was about to start dispersing advice, a sort of crash course à la Farming for Dummies, but I had already heard enough. I told him I had a lot to do and needed to get going. This was to be my personal experience, not some entertaining anecdote to tell his farmer friends around the kitchen table.

One of the things I had fantasized about doing in my new pastoral life was walking into a hen house in the morning to pick up the fresh, still warm eggs from under my very own chickens. The inviting smell of baked eggs and coffee would fill the kitchen as I looked out over my mini estate and congratulated myself for being one with the earth, so to speak. To fulfill that dream, I drove to a regional market and bought a few hens that looked in fine condition to my novice eye. The seller told me that these birds still had a good number of years ahead of them. Great, I thought. My chickens would have nothing but the best whole grains, and they would give me blue ribbon-worthy free range, organic eggs.

I brought the chickens home and placed them out on the land behind the farmhouse. I was busy throwing some of the grains around in wide berthing movements, just as I had seen in nature movies, when I noticed Hendrik observing me from across the way, his hands above his eyes like visors. I pretended not to see him and quickly turned away. At some point in the future, I knew we'd become great friends; just two farmers discussing our crops and harvest. But right now, the competition between a trained farmer and a novice fresh from the city streets was too steep. I needed some time to become comfortable and master this new world.

After another uneasy night wondering about every sound that traveled through and over the old creaking floorboards, I awoke the next morning with excitement, ready to pick my first eggs. Of the six hens, two had died and the others didn't look too good. A few small eggs were halfheartedly strewn around. Not ready to admit defeat so quickly, I concluded that my domestic fowl probably just needed a little time to settle in. I continued my generous grain distribution, but in the days that followed, all of the hens died, one after the other, so that the shovel I had intended to use to work the land became a sad gravedigger's tool instead. When my inquisitive neighbor stopped by again, I was too curious to hear what had gone wrong, so I pretended to be occupied with all sorts of important activities but nevertheless pleased with his visit.

"Keepin' busy, neighbor?" Hendrik asked. It was hard to tell whether he was toying with me or genuinely interested in my rural adaptation. I told him everything was going great, just having a little problem with these birds. He picked up one lifeless chicken ready for burial and studied it for a second.

"Hell boy, you starved these animals to death!" he quickly concluded. I started laughing; these farmers, they think they know everything, No dear man, whatever these creatures are suffering from, there is plenty of food around. Look for yourself, I explained. He was undeterred.

"Have you taken a look at their beaks? You got yourself some retired hens from a commercial poultry farm. They burn their beaks so they won't pick at each other. Those birds couldn't eat all that solid food you threw around even if they had the energy left to pick it up. Here, come with me, I'll show you where our hen house is. You can pick up as many eggs as you like; we got more than we need," he offered.

And so began our unlikely, often awkward, friendship. I spent many evenings in my new friend's cozy farmhouse kitchen. There was something delightfully charming and quaint about the two of us drinking beer around his table, swapping stories under the low light. He undoubtedly had never given the place a second thought; it was simply where he had grown up. The furniture had probably stood in the same place for the last three generations, and his kids didn't look like they had plans to change anything, either. I soon realized that my fascination with country life was matched by his eagerness to learn more about the lives of city folk. He'd nurse his beer and listen to my often-embellished stories of urban life; my adventures with theater productions; the hitchhiking trips through Morocco and Spain. All the while, his mouth hanging half-open, he traveled right along with me. Now and then he would lean forward, asking "Is that right? Is that right?" while his wife stood ironing nearby and smiled her warm, innocent smile, content to see her husband happy with such an odd new friend.

It didn't take long for me to abandon my vocation as farmer; it was enough to observe my neighbor and a relief to no longer pretend to have any knowledge about country life. Hendrik called me to lend a hand when it was time to harvest the hay before the August thunderstorms rolled in, and it felt great to work among these seasoned men of the earth. Sitting with a cold beer in the kitchen after the day's work, tired as a dog and with blades of itchy straw in my hair, provided a satisfaction and sense of achievement none of my intellectual activities had ever given me. Once, Hendrik startled me awake with loud knocking on my bedroom window around 3 a.m. so I could witness the birthing of a calf in his stables. The kids were also awake to help out, and the stable soon filled with the sweet smell of the cow's secretion and blood—ancient elixirs of nature – as a dim light bulb cast shadows around on the stable walls.

During this period, I became hyper-aware of the disconnect of the urban mentality, which accepts without question that food originates in tidy packages at the neighborhood grocery store. Here in this self-reliant world, it was all about feeding – not about being fed. So, between hesitant attempts at writing my first novel and devouring a stack of novels like a glutton at a smorgasbord, I made one last halfhearted effort to cultivate some kind of sustainable life. I sowed a number of seeds that were to grow into beets and tomatoes, plus some basil and mint. The herbs grew like crazy, and I enjoyed plucking the mint leaves for my tea. Looking back at my experience in the country, that was pretty much the sum total of my harvest. When the beets didn't show any sign of sprouting, I decided to dig in and inspect the situation. Of course in doing so, I instantly killed off the perfect process of gestation that had been taking place. I felt like an idiot and wanted to apologize to the battered land for being a neurotic city slicker with nothing to show for my time there but heaps of upturned soil and a chicken graveyard.

Not long after that humiliating defeat, the days began to wane and a cold wind made its return after a pleasantly long, hot summer. I had made it through a full year, four distinctly different seasons, and survived far longer than my farmer friend had bet all his neighbors. One quiet evening, sitting in front of my wood stove and listening to my restless heart, the unmistakable sound of an old Peugeot's engine came slowly up my driveway. Out came my friends from Amsterdam, who had decided it was time to rescue me. At first they were respectful and curious as they studied me in this new world; they too had lost bets amongst themselves about my length of stay in this self-imposed isolation.

When one of them told me that it was time to gather my things and join them on a trip abroad, I protested just a little too much. An overwhelming sense of joy and adventure came bubbling up when, a few hours later, I watched the Peugeot carefully back out of the driveway—this time from inside the car. The light from Hendrik's kitchen still shone brightly next door, and I said a silent goodbye to him with a promise that I would one day return to tell some new stories. We may not be aware, but I think each of us has been given a specific task, and we do the best job of it by living our lives as truthfully as possible. Like my farmer friend, some of us travel the world by working the land and observing nature's miraculous process within the radius of a few miles, while others feel the pull of far horizons and excitedly anticipate the untold stories awaiting them.

CHAPTER FIVE

Return of the Muse

WITHIN THE SAFE walls of my mind and studio, I once fancied myself immune from life's tsunamis. In 1990, I left my native country and with it a promising home in the corporate world. With the act of becoming a cultural refugee, it seems I had forever forsaken the old culture's approval. But then, had I not from early childhood dreamed of living in a place with waving palm trees, where the sun washes away a Calvinist stupor? I left my apartment in Amsterdam as well as all my things—props of a life lived on a different cultural plane. With some cash stashed in my shoes as a down payment on my future, I landed like so many before me in the blinding sunlight of Los Angeles.

For a long time I felt lost, driving around L.A. looking for the center of town, until I realized that seeing any part of town as a center could be liberating in a way. I built a new life under the Southern California sun, and I learned to call this my home. I rediscovered painting and even started selling some. Enough voices in the otherwise overwhelming silence told me to keep going and not give up. Like peeling away layers of an onion, I strove to shed all of the old cultural imprints and see what remained. Life seemed near perfect, but I didn't realize that I had built a home on sand in this new world. I might have changed some of my circumstances, but not myself…yet.

When the mantra that accompanied my journey to the new world, "May all that doesn't belong to me disappear, so that all that is mine has a chance to come to me," finally manifested—fast—my carefully designed life fell apart like a house of cards. The move from L.A. to New York had at first seemed the glorious coronation of hard work and immigrant strive; in reality, it was the starting point of a whole new series of layer shedding. Older imprints, whose existence I had not even been aware of, now came floating to the surface, confronting me with the burdensome weight I still carried from my old world – including a relationship once viewed as the marriage to a soul mate. Later, I came to understand that I was experiencing an ecology check; when we create a vision, our unconscious mind almost immediately goes to work to help us create the circumstances that will bring that vision to reality. I had enthusiastically envisioned a new future for myself, and in my naiveté, didn't realize that most of my old foundation would have to go.

In deep despair, I found a psychiatrist via the yellow pages and walked across the park to the Upper East Side for a consultation. A man in a white lab coat scarcely listened to my account of what I would later recognize as a spiritual and mental breakthrough. He diagnosed it as a breakdown instead, and began studying a list of recommended pharmaceuticals for someone with my condition. I politely thanked him and couldn't get out of his office fast enough. Wandering back through the park on that balmy summer evening, I listened to the birds bid the day farewell and vowed to use this moment as an opportunity. The crater that failed love had dug inside would help me explore other unresolved traumas and injuries and go even deeper into the process of shedding old layers.

I went through a period of wandering the streets of Manhattan at night. I would sit on a bench in Central Park, staring at the gentle ripples in a pond where retired sailors had played with miniature boats during the day, stubbornly trying to reconstruct a life that had forever disappeared. The few times that I wandered timidly into my studio and picked up a brush, I realized I had truly painted from the heart. The cadmium red dripping off the brush now felt like my blood; the brush a surgical knife cutting into my skin. I wholeheartedly agreed with Ad Reinhardt and all minimalists after him: painting was, for now, for sure, dead.

The dry spell lasted for only about a year, but it felt like an eternity. I had cast myself out of creative paradise and truly became a cultural gypsy, no longer fitting in the cultural constraints of my old world and not yet allowed access to the new. Once in a while I'd enter my studio, feeling like an intruder; the paint cans and brushes just sat there, collecting dust. It felt like I was back in my early years, when I had not yet found coherence in the language of paint and brush.

Months later, back in Los Angeles, I still mourned my old life but had come to understand that I had no choice but to grow—reluctantly—into a new one. I found myself rather drunk in a bar one night, talking passionately to a stranger about art. There are many angels hidden among us; this stranger was one of them. "Do yourself a favor," he yelled above the din of the crowd, "Get into your car, go home and paint." I followed his advice and opened up the paint cans in what felt like the biggest audition of my life. When the image started emerging on the canvas that's now titled "Return of the Muse," I knew that I had been saved, no matter how tough my life would ever become again. Whenever someone asks about the significance of what I describe as the New Period, I answer that the difference is I now paint first for me, no longer bound by old rules. Finally comfortable in my new world, I am free to go deep within myself to find.

CHAPTER SIX

Through a Looking Glass

AS A BOY, I always fantasized about being a taxi driver; I could not imagine a more exciting existence than driving around in a car all day. The memory floated back to me one gloomy morning when I was living in my small Hollywood apartment. At that moment, I could find no inspiration for new paintings; my talent agent knew of no quick, well-paid modeling gigs; and during my daily jog in Runyon Canyon—a spot apparently used by the entire Hollywood community as a sort of airing place away from the urban grind—the whispered affirmations I repeated about my paintings one day selling in galleries around the world seemed, even to myself, the mutterings of a madman. But the worst and hardest thing to deal with was the prolonged periods of silence, the total lack of any drama that could give me a sense of direction or function in what seemed increasingly a cold and uncaring universe.

I felt that if, through sheer willpower and courage, one could not somehow overturn one's own material conditions—in my case, the unrelenting arrival of credit card bills and other reminders of the mortgage I had taken out on my future—then life was indeed the hell that Sartre laid out in the existential works I devoured in my late teens. Are we really little more than insects crawling around for a mere blip of time, tortured with minds that fantasize about actually being in charge? I asked myself. If so, I no longer had any moral reservations about joining the army of consumers with their hands in the air, surrendering their plastic to the bankruptcy courts. I would take on some meaningless job—that seemed about the most honorable thing to do in this scenario. Game over. I'd just sit out my time on the planet and forget about wasting my energy running around on some hamster wheel, thank you very much.

But I had not reached the point of defeat yet; a child-like innocence that believed in magic still beat strongly in my heart. There was, after all, always a little more paint and another canvas left, I reasoned. The idea popped into my head on one of those rare rainy spells in Los Angeles, which make the city look quite sad once it's bereft of the usual sun-drenched glamour. With the muffled sound of raindrops spattering down on the banana leaves outside my open apartment door, I looked out into the grey and suddenly decided that I'd had enough. It didn't matter what, but I needed to do something, some kind of simple physical activity, to get out of my own way. But what?

As the memory of my childhood dream job flooded my mind, I found the idea of stepping into another life just to see what would happen strangely enticing. I'd treat it like the preparation for an acting job…imagine the cameras rolling, following you on your journey… So I turned to my oracle of sorts, the Yellow Pages, and found the nearest recruiting center for the most esteemed of taxi cab companies: Yellow Cab of L.A.. I spent a few days on an uncomfortable plastic chair among what seemed to be a mainly Armenian community. It's interesting to see how certain immigrant groups focus on specific jobs and careers: Koreans have their own grocery stores; Indians focus on the 7-Elevens; Vietnamese do the nail salons; and, from my own observations, the Armenian community has taken hold of the transportation business. After a few days of map-reading and taking in basic safety regulations, we were sent downtown to an enormous hall where the exam took place. Since the greatest challenge seemed to be a basic knowledge of the English language, the questions themselves could not have been simpler. I became the proud owner of a taxi license within twenty minutes of walking in.

Now the fun really began. I subleased a cab, sat behind the wheel and drove into traffic looking for a passenger. And that's when I discovered that Los Angeles, practically built around the car industry, is about the worst place to choose a career as a cabbie. All you get is someone too drunk to drive home, someone with a car in the repair shop, or the rare tourist who hasn't rented his own car. After a few days driving through the rain, I decided to take matters into my own hands. With the rent for the cab already paid for, I thought, why not employ a little charity? So I started picking up passengers from bus stops—elderly Russian couples, struggling against the rain and wind, in the Fairfax district. It was interesting to see how different people responded: some would eye me suspiciously and ignore my invitation; others would practically jump into the backseat, no questions asked.

Once in a while, I would get a passenger who had decided for himself that he wasn't going to pay, telling me so in no uncertain terms with a voice filled with hate, pleased to have found a willing vessel for all his frustration. When that happened, I would look at the small Buddha statue that I had placed next to me on the passenger seat and turn up the classical music. I had joined the big league game of fate, and could not care less whether, in my phenomenally desperate financial state, I'd make a few dollars more or less; I just hoped to not get stabbed in the back, literally, on this existentialist excursion.

My newfound vocation made me realize how odd it is to drive around in a city like L.A. with your doors unlocked, inviting strangers to take a seat in your car, with no other weapon than hope that your passenger is not a raving lunatic. But there was a part of me that really enjoyed this new exercise of detachment taken to the street. I noticed firsthand how easily an anonymous taxi turns into a confessional booth. Desperate executives would tell me about the stresses in their lives; their affairs; their teenage children with whom, they felt, they had lost all contact. Some people seemed to have their entire bodies in resistance to the destination for which we were headed. Those riding to the hospital, perhaps checking in for surgery, sat staring out the window, wondering whether this might be their last ride through the city alive.

One evening, just before I was about to end my surreal experiment for the day, dispatch asked me to stop by a motel for a quick, easy fare. A young man with an enormous amount of bling draped around his neck swaggered into the car and directed me with a barely audible whisper to the Sunset Strip. I quickly realized that my passenger was a pimp, checking on his girls. The easy ride turned into a two-hour-long stop and go, and though I had initially been intrigued with my front row seat on the down-and-out life of Sunset Boulevard, I started getting tired and told my passenger I would be happy to arrange for another taxi to come and take my place. "Hold on, we're almost done," he grunted, but I soon realized that his sense of soon was dramatically different from mine. After another excruciatingly slow crawl through the neighborhood, my passenger directed me to a gas station's parking lot, where simultaneously a number of other taxis arrived. Almost identically costumed passengers stepped out and I realized I was witness to a midnight pimp convention. I had had enough.

"Look," I said, "I really have to go now. I'll call you another taxi, but this is it for me." Maybe it was the firmness in my voice, but the pimp seemed genuinely shocked to be spoken to in this manner. He took off his sunglasses and suddenly I saw, underneath the getup and intimidating swagger, no more than a lost boy trying to find his way in a heartless world. A boy who started pleading with me as if I were his father who'd called him inside the house to do his homework.

"No man, I want you; you're my cabbie. What's your name, anyway? Lucas? Lucas! That's cool, man. Just give me ten more minutes Lucas, then we're goin' home, okay?" I was hardly able to suppress a smile.

"Ten minutes and not a second more," I replied sternly as I walked back to the car.

Ten minutes later, I merely opened my door and looked in his direction when he shouted apologetically, "Coming…coming!" We chatted on the way back to his motel about his hometown of Atlanta and his dreams in life, which included music and traveling. He'd love to visit faraway places, he confided. I smiled at my Buddha sitting next to me, and in that very moment, I felt the powerful emotion of a detached universal love for all that lives, even the abusive pimps. We may end up making different life choices, depending on how much we've been mauled earlier on in life; but deep down, we're all children dreaming of a life full of magic and without conflict. We arrived at the motel and said our goodbyes, which, after he realized I didn't know the gangster code, became an oddly formal European handshake. The action itself turned into an awkward ceremony I suspected my passenger enjoyed in some strange fashion as the closest thing he would ever experience to a trip abroad. He handed me an enormous tip—I tried hard not to think of where the money had come from—and told me to "take care now." With that, he disappeared into the night.

The encounter had reenergized me; the car seemed to waltz over the glistening asphalt and I saw the city as a beautiful tableau full of mysterious exploits. Unwilling to go back to my soul-stifling apartment just yet, and curious as to what my next adventure might be, I joined the taxi stand again on Hollywood Boulevard—the default position for the beginning and end of all journeys. I tried to converse in the most authentic cabbie-speak I could manage with my Armenian colleagues, but they instantly detected my intruder status and shunned me like the plague. The rejection made me wonder whether the universe may indeed employ some sort of cosmic caste system. As much as it allows you to reach up in life only to a certain level, it is equally true that if you try to reach down, you will be rejected through some sort of upwards karma vacuum that does not allow living below your natural capacities either.

My taxi-driving stint was merely another in the long line of brief professions I have held in my life: from mechanic at an ironing board factory to stamping time codes on slaughtered pigs; from parking lot attendant to janitor at a convalescent home—a job which mutated into social director if my shift ended early. My career trajectory eventually turned upward, and I became the managing director of an international consulting firm. Now, after my departure from an entire culture, the journey has lead to my existence as a painter in Hollywood. The journey through these professional manifestations had in fact been one long karma setter—fixed lives matched with fixed existences. But now I was on a different trip, one that was about letting go of the fixations. I suddenly saw my daily self-affirming walks up Runyon Canyon as nothing less than a road map to life itself. The vision of a life filled with love, creativity and abundance; a life without pre-set boundaries; a life created in each and every moment. Every single second of my life could become transformed into both a gigantic tabula rasa and a ride at Disneyland. I felt strangely satisfied with the realization that I did not have to fight this natural seat assignment by the universe any longer. With a smile toward my hostile colleagues, I took my cab and returned home utterly content. This had been a good day's work!

But my adventures weren't over. In my dreams that night, I found myself visited by three wise men traveling on camels while I walked through Los Angeles. One of them handed me a beautifully wrapped Tiffany box, and out came a long, finely woven winter coat. I smiled good-naturedly at the nice but utterly useless gift. "Thanks very much," I said, trying to hand the coat back, "but this is L.A., we don't need winter coats here."

The wise man smiled and insisted I keep it. "You'll need it where you're going," he replied.

I awoke to the sound of the phone ringing. When I picked up, the caller was a talent agent from Milan. She said she'd gotten my number from my L.A. agent; I had been booked for a car commercial shooting in southern Italy. A first-class ticket would be waiting for me at the Alitalia counter at the airport, and I was to travel in two days. "Bring a warm coat," she advised. "It's cold!"

I hung up and fell back asleep, only to find the wise man still sitting on the camel, smiling more broadly now, as if he was in on a good joke and saying, "You see?"

Jolted awake, I looked around the empty apartment and grabbed the phone from the nightstand.

"Did you guys just call me?" I asked, terribly afraid I had just dreamed the whole thing.

The talent agent laughed. "What do you think? Of course we did...in two days you're flying to Leonardo da Vinci airport, baby! But as I said, bring a coat. It's freezing here," she repeated before hanging up.

Two days later, I found myself enjoying salmon carpaccio with a nice glass of Verdicchio at 35,000 feet, my new winter coat carefully hung on a hanger by the stewardess. The commercial shoot was supposed to last for only two days, but it turned into a two-week-long affair. As soon as I'd arrived, the weather turned uncharacteristically ugly for that time of year. While ice and rainstorms pounded the walls of my six-star hotel, I slept, read, ate and took leisurely naps. The meter was ticking, though; I was being paid royally for every extra day I stayed in this princely estate. Finally, the sun broke through and we shot the entire commercial in two takes. A day later I was on my way back home. I added the taxi license to my existentialist accomplishments, as I knew that experience now lay firmly in the past. With a generous paycheck in my hands, I could hold the credit card companies at bay yet again for a good chunk of time, and there was more than enough left to treat myself to a generous spending spree in the art store. I was more determined than ever to continue this pathless journey, and, I hope, learn to trust in the creative and sustaining force of life a little more.

84

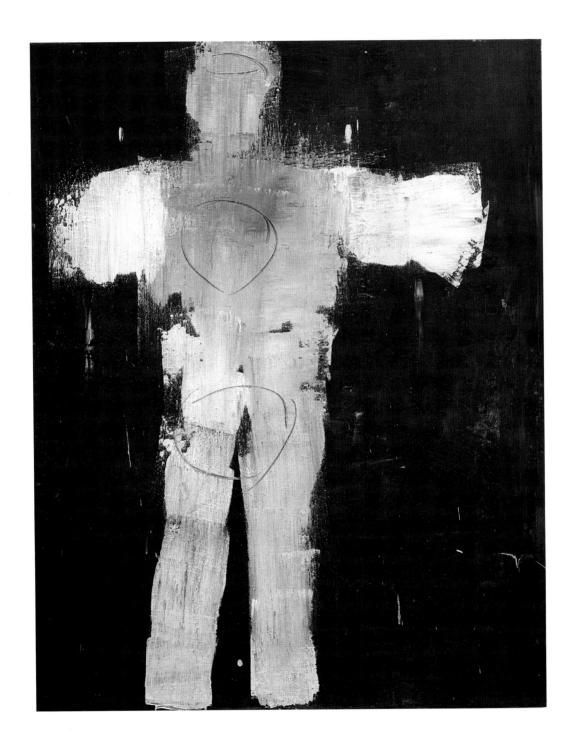

CHAPTER SEVEN

Casino Art & Magic Underpants

THE SMALL, ONE-BEDROOM apartment I once called home had slanted floors due to water damage caused by the previous tenant. It wasn't just a subtle slope, either; it was like living in a ski resort. If I didn't chock my chair with something every time I got up, it would slide, gather speed and crash loudly into a corner. I had turned the little den space into my studio, with paintings stacked on top of each other along the wall of what was supposed to be the living room. The apartment was located close to the Sunset Strip in a predominantly gay neighborhood, and my bedroom faced the street. Shards of conversations, flirtations and fights often took place right under my window, and at night, they would work themselves into my dreams. Sometimes, mysterious gifts appeared on my window sill, such as the morning I found a small statue of the Virgin Mary perched there. A few days later, a loud commotion awoke me in the middle of the night and I witnessed a surreal confrontation between two impeccably dressed men slapping each other with socks. The fight turned increasingly ugly, and at one point, I heard a heavy thud, a crashing sound, silence and then footsteps hastening away. When I looked out my window the next morning, the Virgin Mary lay in pieces on the sidewalk. Easy come, easy go, I suppose. It was a strange, and, in many ways, wondrous time.

My friends and I were all in between places: between careers; between relationships; floating, really. We'd sit around my fireplace smoking small, tightly rolled Indian tobacco leaves called beedies. I had no furniture besides the sliding chair, my easel and a bed, so we used some buckets left behind by the maintenance crew as stools. It was a time of much dreaming; we all felt destined for great futures but temporarily stuck, like stranded passengers in a train that had suddenly stopped moving. During our fireside chats we relaxed and tried to make the best of it, delighting in the exchange of stories that dealt with fatalism, fate and failure. We gave special attention to those events that had almost happened, but then at the last moment fallen apart—the more spectacularly, the better. During this period I revisited Tolstoy, Dostoyevsky and Gogol. I especially enjoyed the wry humor of Anton Chekhov in his "Longer Stories From the Last Decade," who saved the best anecdote from the book flap as an encore following his death. After finally succumbing to a long and drawn-out struggle with his frail health, he was transported back home to Moscow in an ice cooled oyster car...a suitable exit for a grandmaster of the ironic absurdities of daily life.

Meanwhile, as if to mock my financially destitute position, I was regularly booked for modeling gigs that, without exception, depicted a man who has it all: the most exclusive Mercedes-Benz S-Class, Patek Philippe watches, Calvin Klein suits and the like. On the streets of L.A., people would sometimes give me a vague look of recognition, not quite remembering where they knew me from. But I knew. I was an invisible yet iconic archetype. In those days, even when the money and all material security were barely enough to cover the unrelenting barrage of bills, a journey to the studio felt like salvation. As long as I still had some paint and canvas left, the transformation was truly magical. One moment, I'd be sitting on a bucket by the fire, desperate and feeling just one day away from homelessness. Then suddenly, the emperor held court at the easel, the dumpy little apartment filled with an enchanting glow as it turned into a vast palace for the soul. Simply put, the act of painting kept me going and somehow kept the wobbly wheel of life intact.

I had long ago given up on finding interest for my work at the white cube gallery spaces spread out over town. Gone were the romantic ideas that I would receive a hero's welcome when introducing my work to that world. It didn't take long to realize that collectors, the demand part of the market, were welcome there while artists were considered nothing more than little gnomes with pitiful offerings stacked away in their black portfolios. But I kept on painting, trusting that one day, just maybe, someone would show interest. Finally, my luck seemed to change. One of my friends had a friend who knew someone who was a private art dealer and apparently sold paintings by the dozen all over the world. After some introductions, a studio visit to my apartment was arranged. A heavy-set, impatient looking man banged on my door about three hours after the agreed-upon time and told me right away that he wouldn't have more than a few minutes to look at my stuff.

He seemed to like what he saw and commissioned a series of five paintings on the spot for the high-roller suites in a new Las Vegas hotel and casino.

I went to work feverishly; the thousands of dollars in debt that had built up on my credit cards seemed nothing more than a minor nuisance now. The good times had arrived! After a few weeks the paintings were ready, stacked neatly in a corner. When the art dealer returned, his response was: "Not bad, but can you add a little green in the top corners?" I laughed heartily at his joke. When he stared back in dead silence, seeming confused by my response, it sank in. This is the moment every artist has been warned against—the dreaded moment of having to match the painting with the couch. But to be honest, even the fact that someone wanted me to match a couch was a compliment at this point in my nonexistent career. I added a few uninspired dabs of color to the corners, and the paintings were shipped off. I received my check and that seemed the end of a story gone right. The whole episode had somehow changed the dynamic of the bucket séances in front of my fireplace, though, as if something actually succeeding in the real world took the joy out of the fireside conventions. Besides, the apartment manager, alarmed by the smoke coming out of my chimney, warned that it was not a good idea to actually use the fireplace. It seemed I'd hit upon the reason for the sliding floors and water damage…

The casino sale ignited my old marketing brain again and I used some of the money from the commission to print promotional postcards that I sent out to a list of interior decorators and art dealers. Then I set up shop at a local art and interior design fair, which brought in a few more commissions. I was on a roll! One day, in the middle of a passionate painting session in my makeshift studio, the phone rang. The whiny voice of my talent agent told me to get myself over to a big ass casting for a national commercial. I ditched my painting clothes for the upscale-casual attire I had been told to wear and an hour later found myself in a waiting room with a group of men looking suspiciously very much like…me.

When it was my turn to audition, I walked into a dimly lit room where the director, casting agent, client and client's agent were gathered. The director, a young, wiry-looking man, ran up and down the room with unbridled enthusiasm while shouting that this was an audition for Fruit of the Loom underwear; was I aware of that? I was not, I told him, but had no problem with underwear. He laughed, and then asked, "What's that accent? Where you from?"

"I'm from L.A."

"No, I mean, where are you really from?" he asked, undeterred.

"I'm really from L.A.," I replied.

I always try to avoid talking about Amsterdam, the city of my ancestry. Inevitably, I have to listen to everyone's unforgettable travel anecdotes—the times spent in coffee houses, the visits to the red light districts—and it's hard to feign excitement and share in the innocence of another tourist experience. But I could see that Herr Director was getting a little antsy, so I complied and let him regale me with his Amsterdam stories for a while. Eventually, he refocused on the task at hand and said, "So you don't have any problems with taking off your clothes then, I presume?" The presumption was without a doubt linked to the rowdy image that the Dutch have somehow created for themselves, contrary to their overall uptight and intolerant lifestyle. Thinking of the potential residual checks filling my mailbox, and the amount of canvases and paint that those checks represented, I told him I had no problem at all.

"OK then, we're doing a series of commercials with people in their underwear doing all sorts of creative things, like dancing, cooking, reading, and you…" He stood back a bit and studied me for a moment, a hand under his chin. "I somehow see you as a painter. Just take off your pants and use that wall over there as your canvas. Pretend you're working on a painting."

Life imitating art…or…life imitating life? Deeply moved by the dance of synchronicity that the universe had offered up, I took off my pants, picked up an imaginary brush and felt myself diving back into the painting I had abandoned an hour before. I dipped my brush in the cobalt blue and a great swirl filled the canvas over the entire width of the wall. Suddenly, it got very quiet in the room. "My God," I heard him whisper, "I totally believe this guy!" For a moment the imaginary painting session had taken over and when the director called for me to stop, I insisted on finishing the last stroke before turning around. Then we both saw the paint splatters on my feet that I had not bothered washing off. A moment passed, then the confusion on his face made way for a big grin; he understood.

I ended up getting the job, along with my collection of old buckets, paint pots and brushes. On the day of the shoot the production team came to my apartment and, clad in white gloves like a bomb squad touching what no one else dared, carefully transported the entire contents of my studio to the set. They also rented a number of my paintings as set dressing, for which I received an additional payment. In fact, a representative of the agency fell in love with the work and bought one of my paintings. By the time everything was set up to shoot, a canvas measuring 20 by 20 feet was brought in and a battery of fifteen cameras installed all around me. I was strangely aware of the irony of playing an actor who was hired to impersonate a painter. Once I started my painting, the world around me eased away; I was back at work in my studio. From a foggy distance I heard the director's voice reaching me, "Now slowly turn around!" Surprised by his voice, I had trouble tearing myself away from the canvas. When I finally turned, at that instant I truly was surprised to see the small army of a crew gathered around on the set that I'd made my studio.

That evening, when I met up for a drink with a friend trained as a method actor and an acting teacher, I recounted the day's adventures. He told me that my experience illustrated exactly what he tried to teach his students: to be so enmeshed in the reality of the created character that everything else, even the actor's own reality, subsides and makes way for that character. It seemed clear that my personal recession was officially over and that the malfunctioning freight train that had been my life was rapidly rebuilding into a bullet train.

Shortly after the magical underwear experience, my agent rang again and told me I didn't even have to audition for the next project; I had been booked sight unseen to appear in a print advertising campaign for a brand new hotel and casino in Las Vegas. It would be a quick in-and-out flight; a day spent in a tuxedo holding champagne glasses and plates of caviar, a pretty blonde by my side, and smiling into the camera until my cheeks hurt. On the day of the shoot, I flew into Vegas early, got dressed, and stepped onto the tape marks on the floor in one of the hotel's suites. Television sets, couches and beds were still wrapped in plastic like props for a theater show not yet staged. The photographer wasn't happy with the sharpness of the bright desert light and asked her assistant to find a piece of board or wood to use as a filter. A few minutes later the assistant came back with something she'd found in one of the nearby rooms and held it up behind the photographer. "Just make that your sightline," she instructed me, "and you'll be fine." My professional smile suddenly disappeared. I saw something so strangely familiar, but at the same time inexplicitly alien, hostile almost. "Are you ok? Do you need to sit down? You look white," the photographer said as she guided me to a chair.

Pointing at the board, speechless, I finally realized what I was looking at. One of the paintings I had turned in for my first commission a few months earlier had been cut in half, re-stretched and framed. The photographer, who had been an art major before turning to commercial photography, became so enraged that she turned the lens of her camera on the deformed art and started shooting roll after roll to create irrefutable evidence of the slaughter that had taken place. I looked at the back of the newly constructed artworks and there it was—labels with the name and signature of my beloved art dealer who'd given me my first taste of art in the real world.

On my way home that evening, I spoke with a journalist friend who regularly free-lanced for the New York Times; he immediately smelled an exposé. "Think about it...Steve Wynn is opening a museum in one part of town, and in another they're cutting up original art as if it were carpet? This is a great story!" Listening to him, an idea for sweet revenge took shape in my head. I was fairly certain that the corporate heads in Vegas had not cooked up the scheme of slicing up my canvases to get two for the price one. No doubt, this was the work of my benefactor, the international art dealer. His initial response when his assistant put me through was gruff, impatient—his usual charming self. I told him I had just made a shocking discovery in Las Vegas and laid out my plan to him; I would sue the casino for defamation and fraud, and I had a contact at the New York Times who had already showed interest in doing a story on the scandal. As a courtesy, I thought I should let him know what terrible things these awful art haters had done to our work.

I heard some uncomfortable shuffling on the other end of the line; he didn't seem to be in such a hurry anymore. "Now hold on there," he said, "Let's first see if there's another way we can deal with this. Let me call them, and call you back." I find that in negotiations, it's always better to have a deadline looming to avoid things getting stuffed under the rug. I told him that the New York Times was waiting to file the story for their weekend edition. As I suspected, there was no one else he needed to confer with besides his conscience; less than an hour later, he rang me back.

"They're very sorry for what's happened, and they want to make it up to you," he said. When I didn't respond, he continued, "They're guaranteeing a commission of another twenty paintings for their rooms, at a budget of $100,000. I'll wave my commission, so it will be all yours." In one fell swoop, he had just wiped out my remaining credit card debts and provided a budget for the next six months of living and studio expenses. I heard his breath heaving a bit as he asked, "So, then there's no need for a lawsuit or that piece in the paper, right?" I agreed, but thought it would be better to keep up the pressure just a little while longer.

"If they can guarantee the commission and have you, as their representative, sign an agreement and get me a deposit check by the end of the day today, I would be willing to let it go," I replied, as mournfully as I possibly could.

He agreed and promised that a courier would be at my apartment within the hour. Then, just before he hung up, the concerned veneer had already started slipping away as he sneered, "But I'd advise you, if you're so sensitive, you might not want to be in the art business." That was as close to an admission of guilt as I would ever get from him, but it was enough for me, especially since he kept his word and later that day a check arrived with more zeros than I had ever received for my art before.

My friend at the New York Times was a bit disappointed, but I assured him there would be other stories; the art world is a continuum of surprises and filled with pranksters and creative bookkeepers. I didn't deposit the check right away, but put it in a place where I could see it from my easel. Every time I looked at it, I smiled at the irrefutable evidence of the magic in life. If it hadn't been for that modeling gig at the casino and the photographer's need for something to block the light, I would have never found out why the art dealer wanted to make some color adjustments to the work and why he had given the stretcher bars so much attention. All along he had looked at the paintings as something to be cut in half and remounted. It had never felt better to put on my painting garb and get back to work, marveling at how creative and playfully the universe operates.

CHAPTER EIGHT

The Developer

MY DEN DOUBLING as studio, might have been considered charming for a starving artist. But as my art career blossomed, and interior designers, art dealers and collectors started finding their way to my work, I sensed that the successful image that I had studiously cultivated, combined with the prices I now quoted for my paintings, did not quite add up to the environment my clients encountered when they visited. The time to seek out better quarters had arrived, and I soon found an old ranch house in a Valley neighborhood populated with large, fruit tree-studded yards, reminding one of a time when the suburbs of Los Angeles consisted mainly of farm land and orchards.

Confronted with a quadrupled rent, I consulted with my lenders, aka credit cards, and obtained instant, short-term cash. How different from the times in Amsterdam, I thought, when I had to practically go on my knees in front of a banker's desk to receive a small business loan. My gamble paid off enormously from a business perspective. Occupying larger quarters with proper wall space to display my work turned my home into a professional workplace and private gallery, and sales shot up dramatically.

In an attempt to expand my business even further, I signed up for a regional art and design fair in Chicago. With my paintings on display between rug, porcelain, drapery and pillow manufacturers, I felt totally out of place. Just as I considered packing up to leave the fair early and cut my losses, a woman walked up to my booth. She started leafing through my portfolio and told me quite enthusiastically that she was a real estate agent working with a developer on a large new project, and that he might be very interested in working with me. Then she asked for one of my catalogs to show this developer.

I'm often impressed with the elaborate pretenses people will go through just to get something for free, and I labeled this episode as nothing more than the act of an experienced postcard grabber, a species known for showing up at events with empty plastic bags, indiscriminately scooping up everything in sight. During gallery openings, they come disguised as cheese eaters. For instance, at a reception for one of my earliest exhibitions, I thought it appropriate to lavish my potential patrons with gorgeous, catered plates of cold cuts and cheeses. My gallery dealer expressed wry compassion when I first told him of my plan. "You can do that," he said, "but the cheese snatchers will descend upon you before your guests have even arrived."

In the moment, I scoffed at this bit of cynical nonsense, only to be confronted on the day of the opening with a veritable battlefield. In less than ten minutes, the cheese eaters had turned my perfectly presented culinary tableau into the remains of a trough after feeding time. So, as I handed over one of my catalogs to the realtor at the fair, I did it with detachment, viewing the act as a sort of Buddha's gift. Word came back a few days later that the developer had indeed warmed to my images. He let me know that he planned to use my catalog to get a $300 million loan from the bank. "And when I do," he said, 'I'll call you. You're going to help me with the building.'"

A few months after the fair, I had long forgotten about the realtor who persuaded me to part with my catalog. But, as the irony of life often unfolds in less than decipherable ways, this unremarkable visitor turned out to be the person that made that entire trip more than worth my while. The developer and the real estate agent called one day to tell me that they had taken my catalog to the bank as part of a comprehensive presentation, and that the bank had indeed provided the financing. "And now," the developer said, "you and I are in business." He flew me back to Chicago, and before I knew it I was busy designing an entire promotional campaign for the building, with full-page ads in national newspapers featuring one of my landscape paintings. The image had been digitally altered to include a little half-open door in the center which showed a conceptual rendering of the project. Soon after, the official unveiling of the model took place in a gallery surrounded by my work.

The developer began taking me to meetings with his architectural firm—a corporate monolith not used to having artists at the table. I had come up with some clever ideas, such as having the walls recessed where paintings were planned, so the art would actually be in the building, not just against a wall. This would show that the art had been planned as an integral part of the architecture. The developer thought that the suggestion was brilliant, but I saw the architects seated across from us at the gigantic conference table cast their eyes to the ceiling in dismay.

Things took a turn for the strange when the developer asked, with the same enthusiasm and openness, for my opinion about the placement of the restrooms throughout the building and I quickly found an excuse to leave the room. As I flew back and forth to attend meetings and presentations, I noticed increasingly erratic behavior from my developer friend, and one morning, the inevitable call came from his corporate office. I was informed, with cold politeness, that Mr. So and So was no longer with the company. No other explanations were given. Later, I heard from some insiders that the partners had decided to stage an intervention, as my friend's cocaine use had started to become a serious disruption to the firm's business. Naively, I had interpreted the developer's manic intensity as a sign of a creative vibe, something I know all too well as part of my own painting process. As a result of the sudden and untimely exit of my benefactor, my paintings never ended up in the building. But it was fun while it lasted, and our brief association paid for most of my expenses for the rest of the year.

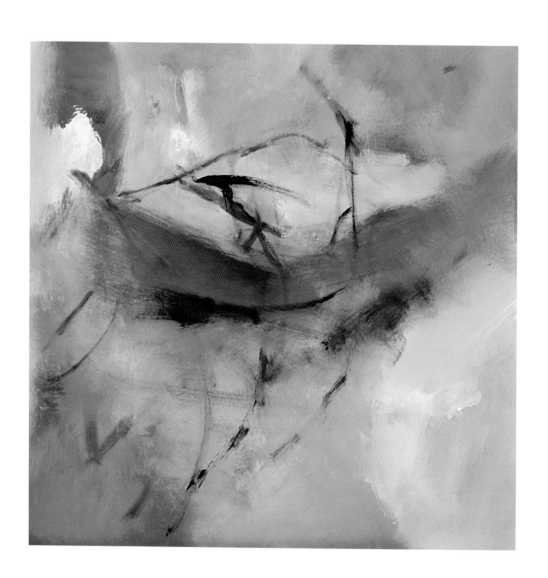

CHAPTER NINE

The Biology of Make-Believe

SHORTLY AFTER ENDING my Chicago adventure, my German friend Wilhelm came to town. I had known Wilhelm for many years, having met him as a sculptor when he was part of an artist collective in Orange County. His artistic career was a shadow in the life he lived in the daytime, though. Trained as a physician in Germany, he had no license to practice in the U.S. and therefore labored in a much less prestigious position – radiation technician – instead. When the work did not satisfy his lust for money or his sense of adventure, Wilhelm became a day trader and set up a mini trading floor in the guest room of his Anaheim home, situated in the backyard of Disneyland's magic enterprises. After almost forgetting to put stops on a few of his open trades, which could have resulted in the physical delivery of tons of pork bellies, oranges and coffee to his quiet suburban street, he gave up on his American adventure. Enticed by a lucrative offer to work for a major hospital in Berlin, he went back home.

Through my friendship with Wilhelm, I quickly learned that while the German psyche overall may be prone to depression and maintaining a stiff upper lip, East Germans are especially marked by an oppressive way of thinking that abhors any inkling of adventure, individuality or entrepreneurship. The world through Wilhelm's eyes was a very tiring place, one in which the chances of things going wrong were exponentially larger than things turning out okay. Shortly before Wilhelm arrived for his annual summer break— thanks to the generous, month-long vacation package offered by his new employer—I had completed a wellness seminar aimed at rooting out sabotaging unconscious thoughts through an integrated process that transformed such thinking into positive, constructive outlooks on life. This process has proved quite helpful in my life, but I do admit that people usually come out of these workshops in a slightly hyper mode, ready to take on the world.

Wilhelm arrived straight from the airport, exhausted, of course, and when I opened the front door, I found him already hoisting enormous suitcases out of his small rental car and struggling up the lawn toward the house. Unaware of my temporarily enlightened and somewhat manic state, he settled in with tales of the latest grim updates on health statistics and the sour state of the planet in general. I gave my friend free range at first, but the next morning, when he asked, "So, how's your business going?" and, before I could reply, added, "I am sure it's very hard to sell enough paintings every month just to cover your rent!" I decided it was time to confront Wilhelm with a demonstration of all that was possible and positive in the world.

I pushed my chair away from the breakfast table and started in on a detailed account that summed up the essence of my seminar. The Biology of Belief, I explained, is the idea that belief systems get downloaded into us from the moment we are conceived by well-meaning parents who walk around with long-outdated instruction manuals. But, hallelujah!, there are ways to override these antiquated beliefs and learn to live life as it was intended for us. My friend looked at me with what seemed like deep compassion, which I took as a sign of encouragement, and so I continued my impromptu lecture with increasing passion.

"It's the perception of reality that determines how the biology of your body reacts. If you think your environment is positive, your blood flows evenly through your body, feeds your organs with oxygen and, most importantly, fills your forebrain with blood and oxygen which supports your rational, conscious mind. On the other hand, if you perceive the world around you as dangerous, your blood flow will concentrate in your basic muscle groups— a trigger placing you straight back into the time of hunter gatherers, where it's conquer or be conquered; eat or be eaten. When confronted with the notion of threat, the blood flow in your head moves away from your forebrain to your hindbrain, where all the unconscious, automatic behaviors are stored. In other words, in stress and depression, you become stupid," I concluded, somewhat breathless.

Wilhelm sat at the table, trying to balance a knife on top of the eggshells on his plate. A small, barely noticeable smile had appeared on his face. As he kept nodding approvingly, I felt I had made some serious inroads into the mind of a staunch pessimist. But the tone in which Wilhelm chose to respond to my talk made me realize that he felt I had not only erred gravely, but was on the verge of a nervous breakdown; someone who needs to be talked down from a dangerously high ledge. First, he complimented me on my newly acquired biological knowledge and agreed with almost everything I had said. Then, with the reappearance of the wry smile, his professorial identity took over the room and he stated, with quiet authority, "If you think you can rewrite any of these commands that went into your system when you were still in a hypnotic state in utero, you're wasting your time. The best you can do is accept whatever they gave you and try to live with it. That's life."

He further explained that in his opinion, I had fallen prey to American naiveté, which always sees the glass as half-full. Meanwhile, Wilhelm felt that he had inalienable proof that life was nothing more than a series of depressing moments in a bottomless pit followed by death, which, by the way, meant nothing more than the body decomposing and everything, simply, kaput. If I wanted further proof, I was welcome to visit his university hospital and inspect some corpses. "There is no one in there, believe me," he said. Sitting there at the table, he looked like a sad but nevertheless triumphant existential king.

I now understand why the recently baptized and proselytized make for the best missionaries. Encountering resistance among the heathen is like throwing oil on fire; the mindset of the disciple is eager—make that ravenous—to provide proof of his or her newly found wisdom. "The proof is in the pudding, as they say, so why don't we run a little demonstration?" I asked. The scientist in Wilhelm perked up, and I challenged him to come up with a seemingly impossible task so that I could demonstrate that, through the powers of sheer creativity and ingenuity, nothing was impossible.

"Remember what your countryman Goethe said," I teased. "If you can imagine it you can create it."

"Romantic nonsense," Wilhelm countered. For a while all was peaceful and quiet in the living room. I looked around and thought that for me, the magic in life had already proven itself just by recounting the journey from my wretched little apartment in Hollywood to this estate nestled amidst the grapefruit trees. Wilhelm broke the silence first.

"Okay, I got one. You know there is a lot of business opening up in China. Why don't you become a professor at a University in Shanghai and, while you're at it, get yourself an art exhibit in the local municipal gallery or museum there. Oh, and let's put a deadline to this; you should have everything in place before I leave, so within the next three weeks." He looked at me with obvious delight, a player who is all but sure of his opponent's defeat.

"You're on," I agreed. "But first, we need to create a ritual that opens up the creative energies and will remind me of my extraordinary powers." Looking around the room, I spied a stack of freshly washed clothes in the laundry basket and wrapped a pair of underwear on my head, like a crown. "I now have magical powers," I proclaimed, and made three turns in the middle of the room. Wilhelm was laughing heartily by this point, which in itself seemed like no small miracle. What happened next left both Wilhelm and me completely flabbergasted. I started flipping through the telephone book looking for the number of the Chinese consulate and, once connected, asked to speak to the cultural attaché. An assistant listened patiently to my improvised pitch about my passion for Chinese culture and my desire to give a series of art and art of business seminars, preferably—at this I turned toward Wilhelm to let him know I was following his challenge to the letter—in the great city of Shanghai.

To my shock, the person on the other end of the line took my proposal seriously and referred me to the Chinese-American Chamber of Commerce. I was to ask for Ms. Lee, a personal friend who as an exchange student had just finished an art history course at UCLA. She knew all the right people in Shanghai and would be delighted to help me. To reach this level of success so fast, without any connections or introductions, stunned me. By this time Wilhelm had wandered off; I saw him inspecting fruit trees in the garden. He would probably come back any moment to tell me about some imminent threat to my flora from a little-known pest that was busy devouring the trees from the inside out. As I removed the underwear from my now-sweating brow, I decided not to inform him of my progress thus far.

Two days later, I had a meeting in Chinatown with Ms. Lee, who turned out to be a fully Americanized Shanghainese who had spent enough time in the U.S. to have her capitalist heart open to inventive ways to supplement her meager secretarial income. She told me that prior to her arrival in Los Angeles, she had been an assistant to the dean of the art department at Shanghai's prestigious Fudan University, and it would be fairly simple to introduce me as a visiting professor. I then remembered the other part of

Wilhelm's challenge: an art exhibit. I offered her a commission for every painting sold in Shanghai if she could produce an exhibit for me in the local museum or municipal gallery. "No problem at all," she replied, her eyes lit up with dollar signs.

The days that followed were filled with a flurry of activity; phone calls and visits took place in which I provided resumes, catalogs, copies of my passport and other paraphernalia. One morning, when Wilhelm and I had just sat down at the breakfast table where our challenge began, a series of beeps in my office announced the arrival of a message. Curious, I got up and witnessed a formal document headed by a number of Chinese symbols rolling out of my fax machine. I had received an official invitation, addressed to Professor Leestemaker, to teach a three-week course at Fudon University in conjunction with an exhibition of my paintings. I carefully laid the sheet of paper next to Wilhelm, who, somewhat irritated by this interruption to the peeling process of his freshly boiled egg, stared suspiciously at the document. Finally he cleared his throat and said, "Ah, well, but that doesn't really prove anything you know."

"I know it doesn't prove anything, Wilhelm, but it's fun how flexible the universe can be, isn't it?" I countered.

I'm afraid this experience may have depressed my friend even more; it was almost painful to see that his perfectly arranged universe of hopeless certainties had for a moment been disturbed. Maybe it made him consider the possibility of gravity being a personal matter, more for one person than another, and that there is a chance that we have the power to commute a life sentence of quiet desperation into something far more glorious? I felt nothing but compassion when I saw him shuffling back to his guest quarters that morning with what seemed an even heavier tread than usual. After Wilhelm's departure, for some reason I could not bring myself to sign the required documents and get my visa organized for the China trip. I suppose I got scared, thinking about the actual consequences of the magic I had created. Then came the collapse of the Twin Towers in New York. With the whole world in turmoil, I found an honorable way out by explaining to my hosts that, in the current climate, it would be better to postpone the trip.

It seems strange now, but those early days after September 11, 2001, had such an eerie quality to them, with few people boarding planes unless they absolutely had to. But to be completely honest, I think part of me used 9/11 as an excuse not to have to follow the process of imagination into reality. Looking back, the lesson learned here was that you can get yourself to a place where magic will start to unfold, but you need to have both motivation and a destination in mind. Otherwise, you run the risk of having a trip with no objective, which is like a life without a purpose. Since that time, I've tried to set my objectives first and then figure out the journey.

CHAPTER TEN

A Very Important Person

AS I CONTINUED to fine-tune a method for the sale of my paintings, I realized that the model of gallery representation that I had set up could be copied and multiplied. I started seeing myself not just as an artist, looking for one art dealer to save and take care of me, and so I turned the model around. I was the manufacturer, so to speak, and my galleries were my distribution network. I modified my catalogs, postcards and brochures to create a space for galleries to put in their own address labels to help them to create a market for my work. After a year or two, I had built up an impressive network of galleries spread out over enough of the country for each to have their own geographical territory and not compete with each other.

One area I felt was missing was Florida, so I did some research and decided to fly to Miami for a fieldtrip. Walking around in the design district, I stumbled upon a gallery that can only be described as a wondrous art palace: large windows; milky white walls; beautiful marble floors; a worn but gracefully aged Rolls Royce parked by the sidewalk like an old guard dog. Walking into the space, one was not greeted with a coldly polite stare from an eighteen-year-old receptionist, as in so many other galleries, but by an authentic and courteous Latin-American elegance, itself a remnant adopted from Europe's fin de siècle.

The tall gentleman wore a bespoke linen suit and thin metal eyeglasses planted halfway on the bridge of his nose, looking for all the world like he had just stepped out of a Gabriel Garcia Marquez novel. He greeted me with a warm smile, and introduced himself as Enrique. As if it should be the very first order of the day, Enrique offered me an espresso. "If it's not too much trouble," I replied, feeling slightly uncomfortable with all the attention and wondering what would happen to this delightfully welcoming mood the moment he found out I was an artist, not an art collector. But when I told him I was a painter looking for a gallery to represent my work, his cordial demeanor only grew.

"That's wonderful," he said. "We've been looking to get more artists into the gallery. Can you show me some of your work?" I pulled out my portfolio and, for the next ten minutes, he was locked in absolute concentration. "Fantastic," Enrique declared at last. "I'm not the owner, but I think she'll love the work as well." I returned that afternoon, and now a whirlwind of energy filled the space as Catalina, the owner, had just flown into town and was trying to catch up on three weeks of business and mail—while simultaneously arranging her hair and petting her poodle. Nevertheless she exuded the same welcoming hospitality.

After briefly leafing through my portfolio, Catalina told me that her gallery director had already told her all about me and that I was a perfect match for the gallery. "We will do a show with you immediately," she announced. "How soon can you get the paintings here?" Dumbfounded, I half-expected the producer of a reality TV show to jump out from behind a curtain. But there was no producer, no cameras, and no apparent money laundering scheme that would explain this quiet atmosphere of abundance— just an elegant man in his linen suit, tempting me with another coffee, and the somewhat larger than life character of the owner, Catalina, who seemed to have taken it upon herself to become the patron saint of all starving artists. I didn't quite know what to make of this encounter, but as I did more research on the gallery, everything seemed legitimate. My conclusion: I must have hit the jackpot in finding a gallery that actually valued and appreciated its artists.

A couple of weeks passed. Invitations were printed; press releases were sent out to various local news organizations; a selection of paintings was picked up and shipped to Miami. A day before the opening, I flew back and received the same gracious welcome. In fact, Enrique came personally to pick me up at the airport in the old Rolls Royce. There was some serious money involved in this operation, and the gallery had collected an impressive RSVP list of art critics, museum directors and art collectors.

A few hours before the opening reception, Catalina sat down to fill me in on the status of the guests and show me pictures so I would know who I was dealing with. Running down the list, she summarized: "This one, he's three billion. This one, recently widowed—husband was in goldmines—worth two billion. This, oh, this is Freddie, don't bother with him; he's worth only 300 million." For a brief moment I felt truly bad for this Freddie, thinking we shouldn't bother him for the purchase of a painting in his sorry state. Then I saw the sly grin on my host's face and was brought back to earth. "Now," she said, "there is one very, very important person. He's one of the biggest art collectors in the country. Very shy, very private; never shows up at any opening. But we hope that his personal secretary and curator will come by tonight. If she does, drop whatever you're doing and spend some time with her. It's our only chance to get closer to the collector himself."

When the time of the opening reception arrived, guests slowly filed into the gigantic space. The work had been installed with absolute precision; the lights on the paintings made everything shine and shimmer in such a glorious way, better than I could have ever imagined in my own studio. Here the work looked utterly glamorous. The paintings were well received by the local art aficionados and I saw red dots appearing left and right.

Led from one guest to the next to carry out the expected "artist chat," I enjoyed the lightheadedness that comes from a larger than life performance. Looking around the gallery, I noticed someone had managed to slip inside who surely was not one of the invited. With his crumpled suit and stained shirt, I guessed the man was close to destitution. I figured he had to be a nameless member of the cheese-eater club—the people who show up at openings to empty the catering table and guzzle free wine, only to leave quickly and quietly as soon as they've had their fill. To my surprise, this person was not headed immediately for the buffet and actually seemed to pay serious attention to the work. I felt with all the success and attention bestowed on me that night, I should be charitable and spend some time with the less fortunate. Excusing myself from the VIPs as gracefully as I could, I made my way over to personally welcome this mysterious guest.

"Hi, how are you? Thanks for coming. I'm the artist," I said. In my benevolent mood, I had decided that I would personally protect this harmless soul from any abuse by the gallery staff. He mumbled something incomprehensible, and then told me it was "nice work." Poor soul. Probably didn't know the first thing about art. "Do you paint yourself?" I asked, thinking that that might explain the man's awkwardness.

"No, no, but I like to collect a little," he replied. It made me smile. I've encountered so many different types of people at openings, many of whom are stuck in their own grandiosity. One such person came up to me at an opening and proudly told me she owned hundreds of my paintings. Hundreds of my works? How was that possible, I wondered, and why had my gallerist not told me? Then she explained. "I bought a book of yours, cut out all the images and framed them. They're hanging all over my house!" It was probably a similar story with this man.

"As a matter of fact," he continued, "I'd like you to come by my place and see some of the work I have."

"Hmmm, I don't know if I can make it. I'm leaving tomorrow afternoon," I hedged.

"Well, maybe on your way to the airport?" he insisted. "I think you'd really like them."

"I'll see if I can make the time," I said, "but I can't promise anything. I may have to stop by some other collectors first." At that point, I looked around the room and discovered Catalina staring at me and making wild gesticulations as she mouthed something I couldn't understand. "Excuse me for a moment," I told the party crasher, now my personal guest. "Don't go anywhere, I'll be right back."

The art dealer quickly approached, barely able to contain her excitement. "That's him, that's him! Can you introduce me?" It turned out that the interloper was indeed the big, mysterious art collector who had for some reason broken his own rules and decided to come to my opening. As the evening unfolded, the dynamic was actually quite funny to watch. The energy had already been set between us, so I continued to treat the collector as someone who needed protection and might be thrown out of the party at any moment. Catalina, meanwhile, was practically licking his heels. I certainly did make time the next morning to go and see my new friend's collection, worth a few hundred million dollars and displayed in a beautiful penthouse overlooking Biscayne Bay. Catalina and Enrique came in tow, and both were treated somewhat indifferently by our host while I received a king's welcome.

In the months to follow, my new benefactor would call and invite me to come along with him and the gallerist to art openings around the country. I found it interesting to see how art dealers treat the people that feed them. The disdain and arrogance that I knew so well from my own time hawking my paintings around the galleries had evaporated; there was only room for niceties now. It was fun for a while, until I realized that the "eat or be eaten" culture held no appeal for me whatsoever. I'd rather do my own thing and feel better running my own art career than being part of a system where the first thing out the window is your creative freedom. My paintings may not fetch in the hundreds of thousands—yet—but at that level the art has become just another commodity, and I prefer clients who purchase the work out of passion, who really want to live with it, rather than view it solely as an investment.

After a while, I lost touch with my unlikely friend. His taste in art was very different from my work anyway. But it was fun while it lasted. And when I glance over ARTnews magazine's annual list of the world's top two hundred collectors, I always smile when I see his name displayed near the top of the list. The gallery dealer, her elegant gallery director, his Rolls, and the gallery itself disappeared as mysteriously as they had come into being. I received a check for sales, and the paintings that had not sold during the show were sent back. There were no explanations; I guess my time was simply up.

Not long ago I visited Miami for its annual art fair. Driven perhaps by a curious melancholy, I walked through the design district until I came upon the art palace that had once broadcast beaming lights like a beacon out into a cold, insensitive world. But as I approached the darkened structure, I realized that only the walls had retained their magic; the building now housed an advertising agency. Inside I noticed the space had been cut up with several cubicles where caipirinhas and champagne were once served to local dignitaries. Like a temple that had been desecrated by the mundane, a row of garbage cans held court where the old Rolls Royce once stood. An old song came to mind then: "Dust to dust, and all that's left are memories." As I walked on through the night toward the area's brand-new development, guided by its ebullient music and sea of lights, I was reminded of how fragile and elusive life, and especially the art world, can be.

133

CHAPTER ELEVEN

Friendly Skies

SOMETIME IN THE fall of 2002, a tourist from New York walked into a California gallery that represented my work. He showed a lot of interest in my paintings, and after leafing through one of my books, set his eye on a small abstracted nude. After some back and forth between the art dealer and collector, it was decided that I would bring the painting to his home for further viewing. Excited by the feeling that a sale was in the air, I agreed. A few days later, I tried to step onto the plane clutching the bubble wrapped artwork under my arm. To my surprise, new, post-9/11 regulations prohibited me from bringing the painting into the cabin, so after many assurances that the artwork would be safely stored in a specially designed, high-value freight area, I reluctantly handed the piece over to one of the flight attendants.

I felt nausea creeping up in me as I waited by the luggage belt five hours later and witnessed the last passengers of my flight rolling their suitcases out of the arrival terminal with no sign of my painting in sight. Grasping the baggage claim receipt as if it were a lottery ticket with a guaranteed win, I quickly bypassed a number of indifferent employees until I lucked upon the desk of a freshly installed PR person still aiming to please. She started frantically calling what seemed a random list of phone numbers jotted on a chart. After rattling off my ticket number several times, her eyes brightened as she hung up and told me excitedly they had located my missing item; it had been placed on the next flight. Too relieved to question why my art had been left behind in the first place, I actually did feel like a lottery winner when the painting arrived an hour later.

My taxi stopped in front of a stately building on the Upper East Side. A light drizzle began, and as a doorman hurried toward me with an umbrella, I felt as if I were arriving on the set of a Woody Allen film. The players: my host, an elderly and long-retired textile baron drinking copious amounts of Beaujolais Reserve; his wife, tall, reserved, stiff and very white; daughter Sophie, five years old, recently adopted from Korea; and me, the artist. The five of us sat around the dinner table under dimmed light as their cantankerous black housekeeper, apparently doubling as chef and butler, all but slammed plates heaped with indistinguishable meat and vegetables in front of us on the table.

The painting, meanwhile, was more or less treated as an after-thought. When some subtle prodding didn't seem to have any effect, I finally got up from my seat, unwrapped the artwork and started holding it up in random spots in the living room. My host delightfully joined me in the game and rejected every placement, as if to say *Cold! Colder! Colder yet!* In one room the wallpaper wouldn't match; in another, the light was all wrong; on and on it went until we ended up in a foul bathroom smelling like the echo of a thousand droppings. I was relieved for my nude when my host again shook his head. In the end, I didn't sell the painting, but I was happy about the way things turned out. This was truly one of my dearest creations, and I felt it deserved a better, more appreciative home than this. The incident brings to mind the words of a fellow artist when I complimented him on the success of his career. "Yes," he said mournfully, as if I had just expressed my condolences. "But it's all the wrong people that are buying my art."

The next morning after breakfast, I walked aimlessly through the city I had left behind in complete desperation just a few years earlier. Now, I took in the bustling street life with the bemused luxury of a detached observer and felt happy. Me and my nude, safely wrapped and back up under my arm, walked though Manhattan without a worry in the world and a heart at peace. Back at the airport the check-in drama repeated itself, but this time I was a whole lot more adamant about holding on to my muse. I told one of the handlers about my misadventure on the inbound flight and begged to use the storage area in the passenger cabin. This time, what appeared to be a higher-up stepped forward and assured me that what had happened en route had been a complete and total anomaly, flying in the face of all regulations and rules, and that although unfortunately these same regulations made it impossible to store the painting in the cabin, this person would personally guarantee the safety of my artwork as if it were his own.

I have to admit, it felt good to encounter someone that dedicated to service, and so, believing in the ultimate good intentions of both people and the universe, I handed over my artwork in exchange for a fresh claim receipt. As the engines hummed before takeoff, I leaned my head against the window and smiled at the sunset that seemed to defy all esthetic rules of color and composition. The moment I got home, I would find a special place for my painting and enjoy it even more now that we had bonded on this peculiar trip. All's well that ends well, after all....Or so I thought.

Hours later, my fellow passengers rolled out of the concrete terminal into the dusty glow of the waning daylight and I once again stood by an empty conveyer belt whose repetitious clacking sounded like a minimalist symphony. This time there were no middle management representatives to talk to—only gruff men in dirty coveralls unceremoniously dumping all unclaimed luggage into an ever growing pile. They pointed to a locked door for further inquiries. After knocking on some more doors it became clear I wouldn't find anyone even remotely interested in taking up my cause tonight. Feeling as if one of my children had just been abducted, I drove home in a daze, too shocked to feel anger or outrage. I located my claims receipt and called the phone number listed to locate missing items. Strange how those courteous, robotic voices on the automated answering system can often seem more hostile than no answer at all.

Suddenly, you've disappeared into the customer service labyrinth; here, every second spent talking to a human being is a waste of corporate resources and a missed chance to generate money. The numbers punched in on your phone in response to the auto prompts identify and tag you as a complaining customer before you even know it, and consulting firms have created entire menus with instructions on how to most effectively get rid of you in as little time possible. That night, while redialing the service number as a numbed reflex, I made a decision: I was the customer who would crack their system and break through their sterile operation manuals. I was that prisoner, unjustly condemned to a life sentence, who would study law and single-handedly bring down the system. They were, I vowed that night, going to pay.

The next morning I sat down at my desk, took out the baggage receipt—aka Exhibit A—and started dialing again. There it is, that same life-less, pseudo-friendly voice on the machine. The object of this game, apparently, is to wear me down until the frustration makes me surrender in defeat. I got it. You are now my enemy and I understand and respect your weapons. I will respond in kind. I looked up the number for first class reservations and dialed that. Within seconds, a very different world opened unto me. I was instantly connected to the front-room, that friendly area where passengers are still treated as if the company actually enjoys serving their needs. I felt like an imposter who had managed to get back into the boarding area, though my ride had officially ended and my time was up.

These excellently trained employees automatically went into service mode upon hearing my complaint and connected me with one of the higher-ups in management. There was that friendly smiling tone again; I recognized it from my experiences just a day before. Only now I was an angry passenger, no longer easily pacified by a memorized reading from the training manual. Then the only slightly higher-ups connected me with a real higher-up, and this person's voice wasn't so friendly. I felt berated as she explained to me in her best teacher's tone, the impatience scarcely concealed, that my item was not insured and the airline did not cover these sort of items anyway. My muse, reduced to a mere item? Where was it anyway? Had some baggage handler taken a look at it and decided it would make for a nice wall covering in the garage? Or worse yet, had it been discarded as trash and lying in a garbage dump somewhere, her canvas and stretcher bars torn up in a irrecoverable heap?

I hung up after wishing the person a less than pleasant day and decided it was time to go into overdrive. Away from the customer service machine; the manuals; the carefully designed labyrinths; I would pay a visit to the boardroom of the airline corporation itself. Oh, the Internet—what a wonderful invention. Within seconds I located the name of the CEO, board members responsible for corporate communications, Statements of Good Governance, Mission Statements, Open Letters to Shareholders, and whatever else I thought might prove useful. Then I called the airport and asked for the name of the person responsible for safety and security. I politely informed him that I was planning a protest march and wanted to make sure I followed the law while doing so. Could he please give me the exact perimeters of the areas that were public property? I heard a deep sigh on the other end of the line and wondered, what civic disobedience or unrest did this remind him of? Had people before me cooked up similar ideas? Then I felt him switching into security protocol position, ready to do the right thing whether he liked it or not, and he gave me all the requested information. When I felt I had everything I needed, I composed The Letter.

This missive was addressed to the airline's CEO, the board member responsible for corporate communications, and last but not least, the Secretary of the Board, that efficient servant who does not judge what information comes across her or his desk, but simply has the responsibility of making sure that all information gets delivered swiftly and to the right source. The overarching tone of the letter, while somewhat mournful, was filled with the authority of a crusader with a strong sense of moral justice and a steely resolve. I provided a brief report of my experiences with the airline and laid out the blatant and serious flaws in their baggage un-security system. I then explained that there was clear evidence that my very valuable, irreplaceable artwork—with a catalog value of over twenty thousand dollars—had been treated with total disregard not once, but twice, which proved this was not a case of God's hand at work but rather, the gaping loopholes in the airline's security system.

To add to the list of insults, I recounted how the customer service drones dismissed my complaints as if I were reporting a lost toothbrush. As a concerned citizen (my fingers were flying over the keyboard at this point), I felt it my duty to let the world know about these abuses by the airline, especially in the light of the recent events of 9/11. I explained that I had already applied for a permit to hold a public protest right in front of the airline's terminal at LAX, and in case they received questions from their shareholders who didn't understand what they were seeing on the evening news, the protesters would be holding up banners saying that this airline was NOT SAFE AND COULD NOT BE TRUSTED with your luggage.

I closed the letter by explaining that unless I heard back from someone within 24 hours to alleviate my concerns about my own and other passengers' safety, (I didn't mention a settlement for the loss of my painting as that would have reeked of blackmail), I had no choice but to go ahead with my scheduled public protest in the days to follow. About 45 minutes after e-mailing and faxing my letters, the phone rang. It was the head of corporate communications, a jovial voice shouting so enthusiastically through the receiver I had to hold the phone away from my ear. In its limitless charity, the airline had decided to wave all its legal rights and award me the amount of…at this point his voice started rolling as if he were a first-rate game show host…FIVE HUNDRED DOLLARS!!!!

I did not respond. His voice, now somewhat unsure, went a notch lower. "Well, what do you think of THAT?!" he asked brightly.

"I am so angry, I can't speak," I answered.

"Well then, what do you suggest?" Wow, his response came so quickly—too quickly, as a matter of fact. He was already negotiating with me. In a calm, neutral tone I explained to him that the catalog value of the artwork was $28,000. If I had sold the painting, I would have received half that amount. I was willing to wave the irreparable loss of the painting itself, not sue the airline for damages, and accept a settlement of $14,000.

"Well, I can't get that sort of money so fast," he shouted, as if we were now discussing a ransom like characters in a kidnapping movie. He then asked me for a three-day period for the airline to do a thorough investigation. If I had any trouble at all, I was to call him day or night, at the office, at home, or better yet, here was his cell phone number. An hour later the phone rang again; the assistant to the Communications Director asked for an image of the missing painting. I would learn later that two former police officers who had become part of the airline's private security team had spent the following two days on the streets of Manhattan with a photo of my painting. They visited all the top galleries to which I had always dreamt of introducing my work, holding up the image of my muse and asking startled gallery owners if they had seen this very valuable painting and whether anybody had approached them in an attempt to sell it.

I could not have asked for better PR.

In the meantime the Corporate Communications Director, getting more jovial with every call *("Please, call me Jim!")*, kept upping his bid until we stalled at $10,000. It reminded me a bit of the drawn-out ritual at car dealerships where the salesman goes into the mysterious back office to talk to the big guy and comes back with yet another, better offer. Jim actually said to me at one point, "I'm sorry buddy, this is the best I can do." I assured him that it was nothing personal, but that I had no choice but to get the protesters and the banners ready.

Twenty four long hours passed.

Friday afternoon, 2 p.m.; five o'clock on the East Coast. Had I overplayed my hand? I wondered. I did not relish the idea of having to recruit friends and visit the hardware store. I'd rather be in my studio, painting.

Four o'clock, West Coast time. I could feel the nervous energy of business winding down for the weekend. The house was quiet. Then the phone rang.

Jim was back, his voice again in game show host mode. He told me that after careful consideration, the airline had decided to award me the sum of...dramatic silence...FOURTEEN-THOUSAND DOLLARS!!!

I did not respond. "Well, what do you think?" he asked, his voice wavering between slightly hurt and nervous, as if to say, "You're not going to reject me now, buddy, after we've come this far together?"

As calmly as possible, I replied, "$14,000 will be fine, Jim."

And that was that. After we reached the agreement, it was suddenly the airline pushing me to be at their offices first thing Monday morning to sign some confidentiality agreements and receive the check. They couldn't wait to have me sign their disclaimer. When I walked into their offices I realized the news must have traveled throughout the company; I saw a lot of heads peaking out of cubicles…Curious faces—not hostile at all—almost admiring, respectful, asking themselves, *Who was this Robin Hood? How did he pull it off?*

I've often wondered since then what happened to my muse. And every time a collector looks at images of my work, pauses before her, and asks, "Is that still available?" I can barely suppress a smile. "No, I think that one is gone…"

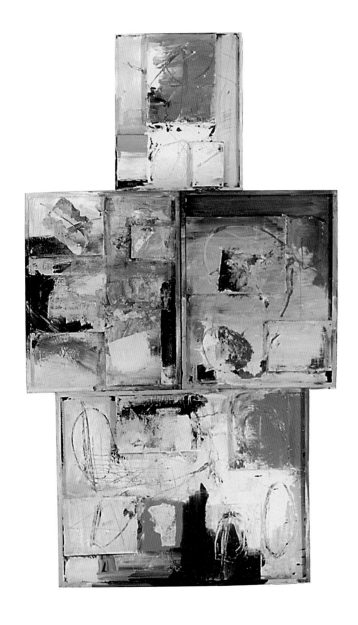

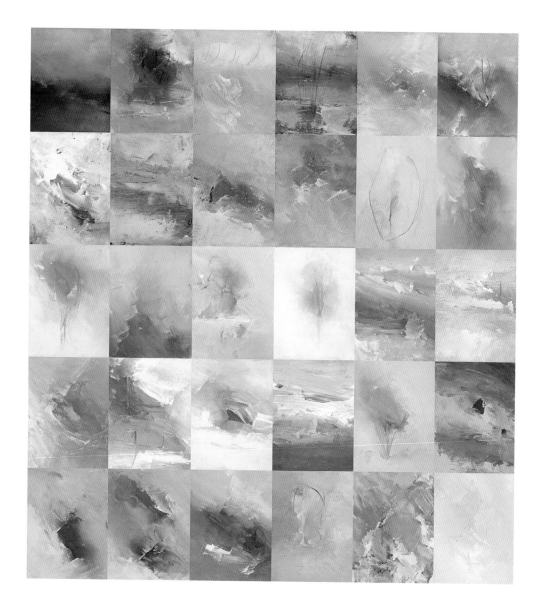

CHAPTER TWELVE

Time

PEOPLE ARE FASCINATED with time. They always ask me, "How long did it take you to make that painting?" One of my dealers gave me a response I believe originated with Picasso: You answer with whatever age you are. It's a good riposte. The physical creation of the art is often the final release of an energy that has been building over time, aging like a good wine.

A similar question deals with 'inspiration.' Sometimes there is indeed the magic sense of an invisible hand moving your own, knowing effortlessly where to put a line, how thickly to apply the paint, and most importantly, when to stop. But most of the time it's a matter of sheer discipline.

To leave behind the world of phone and e-mail and embark on the journey to the studio means it's audition time again. I change into the shaman's uniform of paint-splattered pants and an old ragged shirt. Like a surgeon I briefly inspect my canvases stacked in a row against the studio wall, patient subjects waiting for that first touch of the palette knife, after which their lives will never be the same.

I light the candle under the oil burner, adding some drops of lavender and sandalwood. I'm now in the middle of the ritual. Whether for good or for ill, paint will flow today, that is certain. Next, I make a decision about the accompanying sound. Will I turn on the three-hundred-CD changer, positioned on 'random,' to allow a wild mix of African drums, Bach and Handel, Jarrett's or Haden's cool jazz and maybe even some raspy Dylan or Joni Mitchell to fill my sonic space? Or will it be the orchestra of ordinary notes on a lazy afternoon: the shrieking brakes and revving engine of a garbage truck; a dog barking briefly; a plane overhead…all those strangely familiar, even intimate noises of human life?

Then there is that moment when the humming starts. It takes over all other sounds and is the choir that now commands my hands. I'm back in the fluid world where serial killers, angels, priests and androids hang out as if in some surreal martini lounge. And I'm the mad conductor, willfully creating chaos and, I hope, some balance in this multicolor universe.

A part of myself observes me. At this point, my thoughts are not in charge; they have again become what they always were—commentators on the world. That other world, one of perceived solid and reliable reality, lies somewhere beyond the studio door. However vaguely, I do remember that. But as long as there are paint cans and canvas around me, this is where I breathe and what I live for and where everything, for one brief instant, makes sense. Inevitably there comes a moment – maybe when I've simply used up my energy quota – when the playing is over for the day and I observe the damage done. I try not to judge, but I must admit, I'm very pleased when I see a newborn soul strong enough to move into the world.

 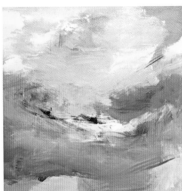 

CHAPTER THIRTEEN

Alchemy

LOOKING AT THE ride that is my life so far, I've come to recognize that the key to my so-called "self-realization" stems from my willingness to say, "I don't know, but let's find out" at the beginning of a conversation, almost as a disclaimer. It's amazing how much more enjoyable life becomes with that simple acknowledgment. The declaration immediately makes you more of a partner than a competitor. With a simple I don't know... let's find out!, life becomes open again, creative and adventurous, full of options and possibilities. What greater gift could a parent offer a child? This awareness has brought both tranquility and clarity into my life, but it is a fairly recent discovery for me. For a long time, I had no sense of direction. I could only count on a dogged determination to get myself to a better place, though I had no idea what that place was or how I would get there.

Having grown up within the strictures of a Calvinist society, I found myself rebelling at the age of 16 by experimenting with copious amounts of drugs, squatting on government-owned property, and making intense abstract paintings with a found pot of black house paint applied to the backs of wallpaper rolls. I made my living by cashing in a weekly check from the government-all the while vehemently decrying "the system"-and by buying and selling old carpets and leather coats at flea markets. Even if it had been brought to my attention at the time, I would not have admitted that I too was following a long mercantile tradition with these activities-an almost inherent part of the Dutch trader's makeup. Nor was it the first time I practiced first-hand the laws of supply and demand.

That exercise began at age eight, when I started going around the neighborhood collecting old newspapers in a box strapped to the back of my bicycle. I claimed the cellar under our house as my territory, and deposited the papers there. If anyone bothered to ask me what I would do with these papers, I told them it was for a good cause. In the evenings, I rolled around in the growing mountain of paper and thought of the fortune I was creating. During one such wallow, I heard the news on the radio of President John F. Kennedy's assassination. Now, when the conversation turns to "Where were you when…?" I simply say, "Burrowing in a mountain of newspapers in the basement."

After a number of weeks, I called a company from the Yellow Pages (my oracle of sorts), to collect the paper, and I received the generous sum of 20 gulden (about $5) for the massive pile. I remember well the pride I felt in my ingenuity and industriousness in those pre-recycling days. I also recall the awe I felt watching an idea plus manual labor transform alchemically into money, which in turn allowed me to spend that "energy" any way I wanted. In the years to come I would repeat that exercise over and over, in different circumstances and with different tools.

After sporadic attempts at schooling with mostly mediocre results, I started getting the distinct feeling I was little more than a small cog in a large wheel that had nothing to do with me. One day, sitting in a classroom with a dated geography book about Athens, I looked out the window and saw a young mother walking on the grass with her newborn. The beauty of the moment and my sense of confinement caused a serious panic attack. I ran out of the building, never to return.

Soon after, I spent some time driving old cars down to Athens, where I would sell them on Syntagma Square. I would use the money to buy myself a few weeks in the cradle of western civilization, inspecting real life firsthand as I drank retsina amidst the ruins of the Acropolis with the local dropouts and other wanderers.

When I finally ran out of money, I returned to Holland with a one-way Magic Bus ticket. Back home, I settled into a life that, despite all my earlier attempts at sabotage, was geared toward full compliance with the once-despised system. But I did not stay compliant for long. This pattern of escape and return repeated itself for years, camouflaged in such a way that it always seemed new, much like the goldfish that can't remember the last time it circled the bowl. A love affair would break up, a job would end, and I was off. With no particular aim in mind, I would "float" through my travels, joining up with a group of actors, or acting and writing myself as I continued to collect my welfare checks. Then I would duck back into the system and resume the role of responsible boyfriend in another stifling relationship, or take ridiculous jobs that required me to walk around in polyester suits.

By the mid 1980s, I ended up establishing a marketing communication company in Amsterdam that specialized in the arts. With an office located close to the red light district, we frequently had to discourage visitors who thought that my secretary, perched at her desk by the window, held the same libidinous occupation as the girls further down the street. In this latest self-reinvention, I suddenly found myself the darling of the authorities. A new political climate had arrived, and the Dutch government felt that institutions and artists had to learn to fend for themselves and spend more of their energy and resources on marketing. During this period, critics were so suspicious of populism that any event drawing more than a half-full theater or concert hall was automatically panned.

At the time, I was dating a British actress who had made a name for herself as a local soap star, and I started commuting regularly between Amsterdam and London. But in my professional life, I again felt as if I were straddling a time bomb that could explode at any time. It got so bad that when I would try to leave my office for a meditative walk through the park, one of my three secretaries would bark, "Where are you going?!"

I found myself sitting in coffeehouses, planning ways to lay off my employees, destroy my company and walk away, especially as my girlfriend started booking parts and jobs in Los Angeles. I felt that this world of so-called success in Amsterdam actually sucked the creativity out of me a little more every day, even as I became a media "whiz kid" frequently called upon to shock audiences as a speaker at business seminars.

In the end, I did dismantle my company in 1990, selling it off in bits and pieces so that I could join my girlfriend in the States. My ticket out, iron-ically, was professional. During an interview with a Dutch symphonic orches-tra, the only strategy I could think of was to persuade them not to hire me for the project. That would only lengthen my stay in a place that had started feeling like death row, as I suffered from increasing panic attacks and pasted on smiles that felt like sandpaper burning my cheekbones. After a cool and detached presentation of what my firm could do for them to raise public awareness and sponsorship, the managing director of the orchestra looked at me and asked, "And why do you think we should give you this job? Do you feel you are qualified?" I finally saw my opening. "You're right…maybe you should shop around. There may be other people much better at this." My plan backfired completely, though. His response: "I like that sort of confi-dence! You're hired."

On the frigid walk through the dark canals back to my office, my assistant thumbed me admiringly on the shoulder and said, "That was a brilliant sales job!" The truly brilliant sales job, however, soon followed. I somehow managed to convince the Dutch orchestra that I needed to do research by talking to the management of the Los Angeles Philharmonic. Flattered by the idea that I would even compare them with this world-class orchestra, they paid for my ticket west. Sales job or no, I did uphold my end of the bargain. The report and recommendations I wrote for them actually resulted in their securing a generous long-term sponsorship.

I packed up what would become the bare bones of my new life and flew out to the City of Angels, where I expected a hero's welcome at LAX from my girlfriend. But one look revealed that the few weeks she had already spent in La La Land by herself, fêted by the Hollywood elite, had made her none too eager to play hostess to a newly arrived refugee. And who could blame her? This was all about survival.

But we somehow stuck it out, in spite of many sleepless nights spent worrying about work and money. I decided to take on the role of 'wife' and help her get ready for her auditions and meetings. After a year of immense struggle financed by a skillful credit card juggling act, I won a green card in the U.S. immigration lottery and knew that I now faced a pivotal moment in my life; come what may, I would stay. Shortly after that, a talent agent literally plucked me off the street, telling me she and I would make a lot of money together. Before I knew it, she had me booked left and right in commercials and other small acting jobs.

In the meantime, I had rediscovered painting as my true love. While my girlfriend slept, I would drive to my studio and paint up a storm. Between acting gigs, I patiently shopped my slides around the L.A. galleries, where 20-year-old receptionists would politely turn me away. As I landed an audition for yet another commercial, the other actors would grouse about the difficulty of finding work and I'd tell them, "No, no this is easy. Try selling paintings...now that is hard!"

After five years in Hollywood, I started selling some artwork and my girlfriend had become my wife and was starting to receive "above the line" payments for her acting performances. In other words, we both felt that we'd made it through the worst. With buoyant spirits, we moved to New York in 1994. From there, she headed out for her next project and I took a trip through Europe, boasting to my old friends about our successful and glamorous life.

In Vienna, however, I was rudely awakened from this false utopia. A fax rolled out of the machine in my friend's apartment across from the Opernhaus. Her well-executed "Dear John" letter included conditions and not-too-subtle threats of repercussions if I failed to follow her lawyer's instructions. Realizing I was a complete wreck, my Austrian friend offered me his weekly session with his therapist. I don't remember much of her advice; mostly I just cried and burrowed my head within her ample Middle-European bosom. When I flew back to New York, the weeks turned into months as I holed up in our apartment, unable to accept defeat. I waited for the familiar click of her heels on the corridor floor, but she never returned. And so I would sit next to the batty old ladies in the park, feeding the ducks and enduring their speculation at who would feed those birds in the winter. I felt so raw, yet so detached, during that time that I would wander the city in the middle of the night, fearing no one and nothing. I came to realize that he who is completely open and vulnerable needs no armor.

When I finally packed up and made my way back to Los Angeles, I felt like a man who had spent a long time in the hospital and now had to reacquaint himself with the world. Sometimes I felt like an emperor, like the captain of my own boat. But more often I felt about two inches away from insanity and homelessness. Until now, I had been toyed with by fate. But I knew I had to reclaim my own skin and determine the outcome of my life. I continued to feel sadness, even a sense of mourning, for a long time, but I also experienced a raw joy singing within me in a voice at once alien and strangely familiar.

Without any sign of impending artistic success, I made the firm decision to be a painter, and a successful one at that. I started visualizing lots of money coming into my life through my art. (As if to mock me, the credit card offers came relentlessly through the mail.) The commercial work diminished, and my mounting bills nearly put me in the position of having to evade my landlord. By now I could never take a "normal" job to pay the bills; my credit card debt had swelled to six figures. To make matters worse, I started experiencing some vision loss and ended up needing a complicated surgery in 1997 that almost cost me my eyesight - a terrifying prospect for someone who had just made it his dream to earn his living with his vision. During that bleak period, I felt like some latter-day Job, reliving that biblical character's injuries and insults.

Yet something interesting happened as a result of the surgery. I couldn't look up for a number of weeks as my eyes healed, so I began experimenting with small 12 x 9 inch canvases that I would discard afterwards. When the recovery had proven successful, I realized I had started painting something completely new. Intimate and atmospheric abstract landscapes had begun flowing out of my brush. It was as if, in the depths of my misery, when there was no place for my mind to go any longer, I had pushed deeper and discovered something that held more power for me than anything I'd ever done before.

Then I came to the last bit of credit on my last credit card. With less than $800 left to spend, my mind started racing. A little money toward rent, a little for food…how could I stretch it out? I saw myself sitting behind my little desk in my cramped apartment and thought, 'Job, Job, is that all you've learned? Now that you've come to the end, you're going to play accountant?' It was painfully clear to me in that moment what I needed to do. Make a commitment. And so I drove to the art supply store and blew all the credit I had left. When I came home, I ripped the plastic off the canvases and opened the paint pots, gleefully thinking 'Now they won't be able to take it all back from me.' I knew I had about three weeks to create the best work I'd ever produced.

Looking back at this time, when I had my back against the wall, I started thinking creatively about solutions and possibilities. Rather than playing the victim, I now started thinking of where the markets were-certainly not in the renovated warehouses and garages, nor in the novelty galleries run by bored, wealthy housewives. With the answer already taking shape in my mind, I drove straight to the Pacific Design Center ten blocks from my apartment and found a willing ear in the president of the building, who introduced me to a few designers. They in turn allowed me to display my work in their showrooms. Before I knew it, a few angels walked into my storage shack and treated everything that came out of that dark and dusty space like gold, offering me what seemed an enormous amount of money for a collection of ten paintings. For me, that moment of crisis, of no return, created the momentum in which the left and right hemispheres of my brain started working together. That decisive moment turned out to be a huge gift. From then on, I walked through the world connecting the dots and finding opportunities that I had never noticed before.

I became a full-time painter-one who treated his career as both a business and as art. In other words, I accepted my self-anointed role as a "successful artist." By acting successful, I started attracting more and more business. And I wasn't faking it. As I saw it all unfolding, I began accommodating this new reality into my life. Although I'm certain many lessons still await me, lessons that will continue to teach me how to live from the heart, this definitely marked the birth of a new understanding of how everything relating to me was interconnected.

I had finally learned the simple truth: no one can take the first step for you. It doesn't matter how large or small that step is; you have only to choose a direction and set yourself in motion. You have to commit to the likelihood that another life out there waits for you to claim it - an alternative that may well be your true, authentic life. Life's energy and creativity can only start moving with you and for you after you make your intentions clear, first to yourself and then to others. If you take one step, they say the universe will conspire with you and will take ten steps for you. Whatever this magical process is, and whatever "the universe" stands for, I have now danced this dance so often that it has become a natural phenomenon for me. This gentle, syncopated one-step no longer makes me shout 'Wow!' but still gives me a deep sense of wonder, joy and awe, making me whisper 'thank you' with a huge smile plastered on my face.

Now, I no longer make a distinction between art and business. I enjoy working in my studio on a canvas as much as I like sitting behind my desk and devising ways to bring my art into the world. Mine has become a wholly creative life, with each facet reflecting and magnifying and ultimately flowing into the others. We tend to create boundaries and separations between the facets of our life, and precisely because of those restrictions, art has lost a lot of its integrity. Art, after all, should not stand apart from the world, but as part of the fabric of society, filling the world with insight, inspiration, tenderness and unadulterated joy. Real art does not need to be protected or hidden. It comes from a place so sacred that it can withstand any corruption. Only when art is made entirely in the world and of the world, as a mere reaction to and commentary on the world, is it vulnerable. Then it does run the risk of being today's hot thing and next year's addition to the pile of discards in the garage.

But no art created from the heart will ever sit on the shelf forever. Even if it goes by unrecognized and unappreciated in its own time, sooner or later it will catch someone's eye who will understand the gift. But this shouldn't be the artist's concern anyway. Whatever the outcome, the artist should focus only on living through his or her heart, on emptying the soul of all clutter and sabotaging thoughts, in order to make the creation of artwork as pure a process as possible.

That is, to live life as a creative being, both inside and outside the studio. In the final analysis, success does not come from the art world. It comes from making life itself the work of art.

I am beginning to realize that I still feel the awe and inspiration I experienced as a child, when I discovered that the combination of labor and raw materials could create a new energy that provided freedom and choice. Only now, this energy is awakening in a new dimension. In art, the classic principle of an economy as the combination of labor and resources no longer works. We're entering the field of quantum metaphysics, the realm not of certainties but of probabilities. What one might consider "wasting" time and energy-a long walk through the forest, followed by reading some poetry and being still for a while-may well yield phenomenal results on the canvas later on. We can never be certain of what is inspiration and what is a distraction. In other words, we're in a place where old dogmas don't work. Only by going back to what was once the first information source, the heart, can we transport ourselves back into a life of magic and creation and become the agents of change and inspiration this planet so badly needs.

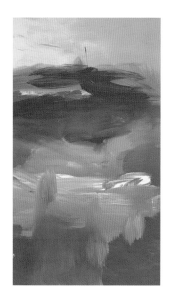

CHAPTER FOURTEEN

Big Phil

MY FRIEND PHIL left today. And somehow, I don't think he'll be back. I think he really was done with this place. I imagine he must be so relieved to no longer have to carry around the burden of a heavy heart. Ever since he announced the passing of the love of his life, I think he signed off from his own as well. From that moment, he had moved around in a sort of suspended daze; a man who saw life as nothing more than an uncomfortable waiting room. I received a call with the news while in the airport lounge. How appropriate. He left early this morning, slipped out the back door…pretty much the same way he would leave parties. He left just a few hours ago so he can't be that far yet, but I can't catch up with him now, even if I try. It's not like he's just cruising down some country road with the windows of his old black Mercedes rolled down to enjoy the warm breeze as it plays with the unruly curls on his head…It's not like that.

The first time it dawned on me that Phil might soon travel by a different means of transport was when I visited him at the hospital. Since his stroke, he could no longer open his eyes. He tried—I saw his eyelashes flutter—but it was as if life had become too heavy for them to absorb the physical spectacles of the world. His spirit was still there, though. I know because when I sat with him, offering up my review of the latest Woody Allen film, he responded with his beautiful signature smile. That large warm hand resting in mine made me feel exactly the same as when we congregated every six weeks or so at Musso and Frank, aka our clubhouse, for lunch. Sitting in a booth reserved just for him always made me feel like we were in on a joke together. For more than fifteen years we met up at this place, one of the last Hollywood holdouts, hiding from the tourists outside and their digital cameras snapping in rapid fire like machine guns. We always ordered the same: sand dabs for him, an avocado mushroom omelet for me. To the waiters he was known as Big Phil, an honorary name Burt Lancaster once gave him when they worked on a film together. Phil was such a celebrated customer that he even had an open tab at Musso's, like in the good old days. But the waiters never warmed to me. If I arrived early for one of our get-togethers, I'd say, "Hi, I'm here for Phil," and point at his booth.

"Mister Phil" the headwaiter would correct me, and he had no qualms about having me stand there like a school boy while I waited until the boss himself arrived. I cannot imagine ever walking into that restaurant again. Being there without Phil, staring at his booth with someone else seated there? I don't think so.

Phil came into my life when I was still married and had just moved to L.A. He recognized my wife from a BBC sitcom she had worked on before we left for Hollywood, and we became friends almost immediately. It gave him great pleasure to introduce me to some almost invisible places that are actually the cultural icons of this city: Musso and Frank, the Magic Castle, The Pantry downtown, The County Museum, Huntington Gardens in San Marino, with its prized Blue Boy by Thomas Gainsborough and a number of great Constable paintings. He would come down to my studio downtown, curious to see new work, and always had something encouraging to say about the evolving paintings. When my marriage fell apart and the pieces shattered in a fairly ugly way, I holed up for a while in the apartment in New York—a place that, only a few months earlier, it seemed a new and glorious life of marital bliss had sprouted. When I finally made it back to L.A. with my tail between my legs, the first thing Phil did was arrange a lunch for us at Musso and Frank, assuring me I had as much right to be there as anybody else. It felt as if he were the mayor, handing me the keys to the city.

Even the mention of my ex's name would make my heart cringe, so Phil started calling her The Situation and continued to do so for years to come. Eventually it became a running joke, even long after the mourning pains faded and I had found a new love, whom Phil clearly not only approved of but adored. He would bend across the table at our lunch and whisper conspiratorially, "I wonder what The Situation would think of that." A few months before he left, he came to lunch at the home I've built with the new love of my life. The house sits gloriously on top of the Hollywood Hills—the famous sign is practically in our backyard—and serves as an enduring reminder to believe in magic. Phil followed me on a tour through the house, looking around like a building inspector, and finally said approvingly, "And that's what you have built, all with your bare hands. Think about that!" That was vintage Phil, always trying to convince me of my own qualities.

A quiet man, most comfortable in the background, Phil Norman achieved enormous success as one of the most celebrated title designers in the history of film and television after coming out from the Mid West in the 1960s. Devastated by the loss of his partner, and ultimately phased out by new title companies and design studios after the switch from analog to digital media, I pictured Phil roaming the bookstores, leafing through film encyclopedia to read about long forgotten stars. Just names for many others, these were living memories of personal contacts for Phil; people with whom he'd spent many afternoons on Hollywood's studio back lots. He did most of the titles for Sidney Pollack's movies, and, deeply shocked when he heard of Pollack's death, told me that they'd met just a few weeks earlier in the dairy section of a local supermarket. I could just picture it: two old bears, their tall bodies hunched over shopping carts while discussing the state of affairs of Hollywood.

The thing that troubled me the most when I went to visit him for the last time was that his shoes had been taken out of the room…and his eye-glasses weren't there either. What if he woke up and felt like walking around a little, or maybe wanted to read the paper and went to reach for his glasses on the nightstand? A child-like anger came up against cold logic: you really can come to a point in life where options are no longer part of the process. That's hard to accept. The road might have gotten narrower for Phil for a while now, but I had never thought about an actual end.

The last time we met for lunch at Musso and Frank, at some point between the sand dabs and the flan, he looked over at me and said quietly, "Don't give up on me yet…I may still have another act in me." As far as I was concerned, when I heard that, his journey of the last few years had been nothing more than the painful but inevitable comeback of Big Phil.

When the voicemail came through at the airport with the message that he had gone, I at first felt fine. It was his choice after all; stay or go, what's the difference, I thought, you live in my heart anyway. I was surprised at how easy it seemed to deal with someone's departure. But later, as I looked out the window to study the cumulus clouds from above as Constable had done before me from below, a deep sadness starting setting in. I realized that I was going to have to do without that warm smile for the rest of my life. Though I know exactly how he would respond, and I can just picture him sitting here right next to me, slowly nodding his head, always showing empathy and understanding, whatever I'd tell him. That was Phil's greatest quality: All the things he did not say. The calm understanding and nodding grins. No judg-ment ever. It made me realize that it is not the big talkers that leave a void. It's the quiet men, the ones who never judge but are always there, silently filling the world…those are the ones whose absence leaves the biggest crater.

CHAPTER FIFTEEN

Emails to a Young Artist:

[HOMAGE TO RAINER MARIA RILKE]

Dear Elsa, thank you for your email...

Yes, it was a wonderful dinner indeed. I enjoyed meeting your parents, coming straight off the plane from L.A., traveling to Germany, and then back to Switzerland. Later I realized I had been shuttling between the two cities where psychoanalysis was born and where the "big guys" like Freud and Jung got together attempting to crack the codes to get access to the unconscious. You're choosing an interesting path to get to your art (heart). As long as you don't get lost getting there, it might be a good idea, especially if you want to work in the art business.

When I teach, I focus on giving artists communication and marketing skills, to help them become independent and empowered. The reason that so many artists are not very good in marketing their work is, I believe, mainly biological. There are left and right hemispheres of the brain, and if you focus on developing only one side, the creative part, the other is going to suffer... So in a way, if you keep feeding both your creativity and your management skills, you will be way ahead of others who want to work in the creative field...

Dear Elsa, it was lovely to hear from you again.

I'm writing to you from the lobby of a hotel/casino in Memphis, Tennessee. I did a large commission for them and had to come by to inspect the installation and do some touch-ups on the work. Seeing people gambling their money away is quite a depressing sight. It would be so much better if people were in touch with their creative powers and wouldn't have the feeling they have to gamble to get lucky.

You raise a few very important points in your message. Let me assure you that you are not crazy, and that dreams are the most important capital for a creative person to tap into. Always be careful with whom you talk to about your dreams; most people would rather shoot them down than encourage you. That is no reflection on you—that's just their own sorry state. Remember, it was your countryman Goethe who said that everything you can dream up, you can realize. I came from a small town in Holland and as a little boy dreamt of palm trees. I held on to my dreams and now see them every day driving along the freeway. They tested me in school and thought my best chances were to become a certified accountant. It just shows you... you can only trust your own dreams, and learn to work with the tools that will help you to realize them.

We look at the world through our conditioned minds, and it is pivotal to come to the understanding that most of what we think is based on information that originates from the Dark Ages. You can't trust your mind until you clear out the viruses that are thrown into it from early on. The creative heart needs to be the boss – the rational mind its assistant... From your words I understand that you are looking for a way to get in touch with your creativity and live from that place. I commend you for your investigative spirit! I understand your trepidation of the big city... L.A. is a challenging place. But for someone with a dream it's a very rewarding place. It is the city of dreams after all. Keep your heart alive....Keep dreaming... Whatever your mind can dream up, it can realize....

Dear Elsa, thanks so much for your last email.

I'm sorry it took me a while to respond. I was traveling, had the opening of a large retrospective exhibition of work (over the last fifteen years) with my gallery, Galerie d'Orsay, in Boston. Am now back, and with no traveling plans for the month of August. I'm very much looking forward to being home, spending time in the studio, and maybe even going to the beach sometime. L.A. is a wonderful vacation destination, but it's always a challenge to take time off in your own city...

You make a few keen observations about art, career and life. I agree with you that no matter what career you choose, it's going to be a challenge. So I therefore argue that it is much better to choose the career and the work that you love so that your struggle has meaning. What a terrible idea, to work hard for something you don't even like... I am convinced that whatever it is you set out to do, you can make it into a success. But it takes inspiration, love, persistence and patience. Like growing a seed into a large, healthy plant—you don't expect the result overnight—you build it, nurturing step by step, day by day. With all the people complaining how hard it is to have a creative career, whether it be a writer, a poet, a dancer, singer, actor or painter, I always ask: How much time do you actually spend being in love with that which you think you want to do? How much time do you spend studying the field, make yourself familiar with it, doing research, and above all: DOING IT? How many hours a day do you write, or sing, or dance or paint?

Most people are waiting for permission. But once you park yourself into the waiting room, you will be stuck there for the rest of your life. Because the only one authority that is going to give you permission to do what you want to do is YOU. That's why I'm highly suspicious of institutions and schools teaching art... Most of what they do is un-teach; get you afraid, make you into an intellectual being that has to rationalize every step, while forgetting that it is the heart that is the true teacher.

There used to be a great educational system in place, especially in your country, of apprenticeship. (Herman Hesse writes a lot about this in his novels). They understood in those days that there are different periods for the mind to learn and expand. So, after a period of schooling, you were kicked out of the nest and started traveling the world, learning by spending time in the physical presence of the masters who had the professions you were interested in, whether it was sculpting, painting, textiles, shoemaking or whatever... Then, when you had swept the floors for a while in their studio and observed the whole process of their life and work, you came back to school to further cement the information, but based on your own experience and knowledge. Nowadays, there is such an emphasis on the intellectual process that most university graduates have a head stuffed full of ideas without the muscles necessary to be a creative leader and bring those ideas into practice. That unfortunately creates clerks, not creative artists. So I'm glad to read that you have your doubts about the institutions, and I'd say that it is a very healthy doubt.

Why is it so difficult to find ourselves, to become in charge of our lives, and not feel like a malfunctioning robot? In new cellular biological research, more and more information is found that points in the direction of early childhood, and even the period in the mother's womb. It turns out that the building of a fetus' mind, works pretty much the same way your computer downloads software into its system. And you know how easy it is to get a virus in your system or have the system malfunction if the downloading is interrupted.

The same goes for the downloading of information from the "mother brain" into the "fetus brain." We are not blank slates when we come into the world; our brains have already been wired with all the frustration, the anger, the shortcomings of many generations before us, and with ideas about survival that may have made sense two hundred or two thousand years ago, but not for the digital age... So our job is, if we want to find out who we really are, without all the fillings of parental values and morals and cultural rules and set values by society, to undo all these external rules and values, and find our own. Once you get into that domain there is a huge storage room of information and creativity and resources available that will help you to find your way. No longer having to buy into and feed all those generations before you, (who in the end have absolutely nothing to do with who you are), you are no longer wasting your energy, and you can run on the eight cylinders you were given at conception, instead of the two cylinders most of us end up running on.

Of everything in my life, I've found that following that process and path of introspection and investigation is the most rewarding path for an artist. And by artist I mean doing that which you are in love with, that holds a personal relationship that you create yourself: unique, in other words. What you do with that creativity is totally unimportant: you can become a sculptor, a painter, or jockey or bookkeeper, or window washer. Whatever the shape, if it comes from a place of passion and love, it will make you an artist...

⊷⊜│⊜⊷

Dear Elsa, thanks for your last emails.

Yes, I agree, the U.S. is not the place where culture is born... But it is the place where dreams can come true. I would just want to say this: Your motivation expressed in your last emails for wanting to continue business school sounds fine, but I'm just missing one element. What is your dream? What is your passion? I know that it is hard to protect yourself from the onslaught of society that wants you to look at the world in a material way... something that feels safe, that holds up the promise that it will protect you. But if you don't follow, or at least try out, what it is that your dreams tell you, then what value does life have at all? Maybe, when you're done with schooling and you have your degree, it might be good for you to "get lost" for a little while. Let the heart tell you where to go... Allow yourself to not know and find out... The mind likes to play tricks with us, and offers the illusion that everything can be sorted out through a thinking process.... This is a sad misconception that creates a lot of chaos and destruction in the world. It is the heart really that rules, and that you should always trust... The heart is always right; even when it's wrong, it's right...

So my advice: Look out for what Elsa wants, pay attention to what her dreams tell her when no one is around to try and push her into thinking in terms of security...

Follow your dreams and find out where they lead you. Ultimately, that's the only real safe place to be in life...

Why the Next Renaissance May Be Around the Corner

ONE OF MY most treasured collectors and his wife flew in from the East Coast to see me recently. During challenging economic times, people will easily find reason to place a moratorium on art purchases; for many, it is the very first thing to go. But this passionate collector was eager to come to my studio as soon as their plane landed, and he had me set aside six paintings. "I love them all, of course," he explained, "but these six are really jumping out." I felt like I had to talk him down a bit, reason with him like you do with an addict, for this was not the first painting he was looking at; he was about to add to a sizeable collection spanning different periods of my painting career.

"Times are a little tough right now," he continued, somewhat apologetically, "so I can only buy two or three this time." This is by no means an irrational person. On the contrary, the man is about as disciplined as they come. After a career on Wall Street as an investment banker and financial analyst, he now has his own firm and handles portfolios worth hundreds of millions of dollars. His explanation for not getting burned in the recent financial crisis was simple: "I know I'm a pretty smart guy, so if I didn't understand those derivatives, I wasn't going to advise my clients to deal in them either."

Whereas for other patrons, I tidy up my house and studio and select but a few paintings for them to see so as not to overwhelm them, this collector goes through my entire collection with raucous vigor and delight—and a very keen eye. He is one of a small group of angel collectors that have purchased my work over the years, and that keep me inspired to continue painting. They give me the courage to speak in front of collectors and art aficionados, and to deal with the press. It's as if I can almost hear his warm, unpretentious voice telling me, "Just be who you are, it's more than enough."

These collectors, who keep purchasing and surrounding themselves with art, understand that art is not just a luxury that you acquire when all other impulse purchases and toys have been exhausted. Through personal experience they understand that surrounding oneself with art, whether in the home or office, can positively affect the creative mind, their outlook on life, and their actions. In other words, surrounding yourself with art can make you smarter, and, as a result, may help you make better decisions that ultimately have a positive effect on your finances. And that is just the material result. Numerous studies point out that surrounding yourself with art that you love can greatly reduce stress levels, lower blood pressure or help improve digestion. Art is even used as a color map in Alzheimer clinics, since color coordination is stored in the deepest areas of the brain and can still be accessed long after other cognitive capacities have stopped functioning.

One of those angel collectors appeared out of thin air at another crucial moment some fifteen years ago. After having painted for many years without enough recognition and sales to sustain an art career, financial pressures forced me to keep my finished canvases in a storage unit. Just when I felt I had reached the end of my rope, an interior designer saw one of my paintings in a showroom, did a dramatic pirouette, and, with a classic "Mon Dieu!," insisted on a visit to my storage unit. He drove up in a roomy Range Rover with his partner and together they treated everything that came out of the dusty vault as if the chambers of a newly found pyramid had just been unearthed.

Over the years, these passionate individuals have shown up, seemingly out of nowhere, and grown to a sizeable army. They may not be aware of it, but it is these people who always appear at exactly the right moment, as if to say, Don't give up; stay loyal to your dream. An important lesson I've learned over the years, having dealt with the wild fluctuations and roller coaster ride the art world can be at times, is that if you stay loyal to your dreams, life will always sustain you. It may not always be comfortable, and you may have to let go of things you thought you would never have to leave behind, but I've learned that the process ultimately leads to a better place and a richer life. To paraphrase Mick Jagger, You can't always get what you want, but if you try sometime, you may get what you need. One of my collectors taught me to always say, no matter how bad or wonderful a juncture you find yourself at in life, "Things are not as bad as they actually are; the best is yet to come." I hope to be able to say that on my deathbed...I guess that would be the ultimate test of trust.

The East Coast collector and his wife organized their stay in Los Angeles around a daily inspection of the paintings, until four lucky contenders emerged. During their visits to the studio they fell in love with my coffee, which comes from an Italian percolator. The process takes some time; the pot sits on the stovetop and the Old World ritual of waiting for the water to boil and work itself through the pressure chamber comes into play. Sitting around the kitchen island, listening to the comforting sounds of simmering coffee, the collector's wife started asking me questions about my life. Keenly observant, she had filed away every comment, no matter how minor, I had made during our time looking at the work in the studio. She was very specific—wanted to know every single detail—as she clearly related and spun a path from my earlier experiences in life to the place I had now reached. Funnily enough, her questioning brought up and linked events I had completely forgotten about. As I told a few stories that had significant meaning for me on my journey in becoming an artist, she stared in disbelief and asked, "Are you making all that up?" She kept repeating the question, forcing me to take another hard look into my memory bank. Aside from some unconscious editing that the mind naturally does, my experiences were all factual realties. I suddenly realized that if she thought I'd made it all up, I might be walking around with some interesting material in my head.

My collectors eventually made their final decision, added two paintings to their collection and left town. Soon after, my partner and I had dinner with two seventeen-year-olds who had just finished high school. One had already decided on the next leg of his journey and was to start art school in the fall, but the other one wasn't so sure. To the alarm of her parents, she had decided she might want to take a little break from institutions and discover life on her own for a while. It brought to mind a statistic I recently read: some 80% of art school graduates never touch art materials or make art again within two years of graduation (other than ending up behind the counter of an art supply store perhaps). Her decision to sort out what she actually wanted in life was perhaps not the waste of a good education that her parents feared. To me, it seemed healthy and courageous to want to take a look at the world and test her interests against the tapestry that's out there so she could make a truly informed choice of what field to focus her studies on.

Listening to the teen's frustrations, observing how her healthy curiosity had to do battle with well-meaning parents who felt she was squandering her precious youth, made me realize that while the world is changing rapidly before our eyes, we're still walking around with concepts that are completely outdated. An educational system that favors the intellectual, rational part of the brain over the intuitive, creative side—even in art schools—may have been a good reflection of the times during the Industrial

Revolution, but we have now entered the Information Age, where requirements for successful participation are dramatically different.

Easy access to information and creative tools available through electronic and online media means we now live in a time in which clear boundaries between the "creative mind" and "business mind" are blurring further and further. Identifying individuals biologically, with terms such as right brain thinker (one who uses the intuitive, creative part) and left brain thinker (traditionally called the more rational operator) has become increasingly obsolete. In the new world, a creative mind is the winner in every environment, whether it be scientific research, the arts, or in the business world. Unfortunately, the current educational system is not equipped to deal with curiosity as an asset instead of a nuisance. And creativity loves empirical experience; not textbooks that explain them. Yet, when you think of the positive consequences of dealing with life itself in a less fixed, more flexible way, one might wonder whether billions of dollars could be saved and used in more constructive ways. A company like General Motors might be in a lot better shape today if more innovative thinking had been adopted early on.

When discussing this with my collector, the former financial analyst, he explained that in his experience, the corporation that encourages experimentation and, on a controlled and limited scale, views failure as a valuable lesson from which to learn, is the corporation that is able to adapt, stay competitive and enjoy success in the long term. The monolithic conglomerates that use their R&D departments to design better locks on their doors, meanwhile, will eventually crumble and bite the dust.

Another interesting perspective on the times we live in, and its requirements for survival and success, is offered by the authors Alvin and Heidi Toffler in their recent book, *Revolutionary Wealth*. They argue that in every organized society, from the first agricultural communities to the highly organized Industrial Age, economies were based on finite resources. As resources grow scarcer, prices rise, and ultimately, as M. King Hubbert argued in 1956 with his coined phrase "peak oil," society reaches its crescendo and then plummets until nothing but interesting artifacts remain for curious archeologists to dig up centuries later.

In his book *Collapse: How Societies Choose to Fail or Succeed*, Jared Diamond provides numerous examples of what seems to be an almost iron law of rise and fall. It is an interesting coincidence that the new economies, with a giant like Google being a pointed example, are driven by information, and that the new fuel—the gold of the future—is found in natural resources: sun, wind and water. These natural resources have an important trait in common with the new capital resource of information: both are a much more fluid and flexible material, and therefore very different in substance from their predecessors. After use, oil and coal have nothing but waste to offer; they endanger rather than enrich the planet. Information however, as the Tofflers reason, begets more information and leaves no pollution in its wake.

But are we ready to deal with this radical change? Are we ready to consider that it is no longer efficient to use the brain's memory bank to store fixed data; we should instead use it for navigation and creative thinking, as we can now Google any question and access any data we seek? Surrounded by undeniable evidence that our visit to this planet is, in evolutionary terms, nothing more than the overnight stay in a bed & breakfast, why do we insist on setting up shop as if we are here to stay indefinitely? By treating our own house—the body—with permanent actions such as surgery instead of applying proven, ancient eastern methods like acupuncture to release blocked energy and create flow again, it seems we are scared to death of looking at life for what it is: a river in a constant process of evolution and change. We seem so afraid of learning to appreciate the beauty of life's impermanence. And why is it so hard to find our original creative voice? Some dramatic and interesting answers to these questions have come up in recent years, many from the field of cellular biology.

Before exploring these findings though, we have to go back in time. The true revolution in science, the one that, very quietly, turned the world on its head, happened some hundred years ago with the discovery of quantum mechanics and Heisenberg's Uncertainty Principle, which demonstrated that there is no such thing as objective research. The mere presence—and attitude—of the researcher influences the very behavior of the object observed. Unfortunately, not much has come out of these revolutionary discoveries other than the availability of unfathomable destruction in the form of the atom bomb. If the academic community was less obsessed with the race to publish their research, or with who is short-listed for the Nobel Prize, they might rethink the strict hierarchical structures that isolate the individual researcher from having open debates between different departments that might lead to some interesting findings.

An interdepartmental détente might also help students better prepare for a world that is becoming less fixed by the day, with all manner of information increasingly available at one's fingertips. Why does this rigidity often exist in institutions where you would most expect an open mind? Why the fear of change in the face of the ever-changing flow of the river of life? Although at this time the momentum is still firmly on the side of old, rigid ways of thinking, there are interesting developments in certain areas which I hope will, sooner or later, be allowed out of the fringes to form part of a healthy, vigorous study and debate. Case in point: I recently spent a wonderful afternoon with the administrator of Harvard University's new neuroscience department, which has purchased one of my paintings. Here, it seems a serious attempt is being made to encourage debate between different disciplines.

Likewise in the field of cellular biology, where a minuscule part of available research budgets is now used to study environmental causes of behavior, rather than solely support the gigantic gene machine and the pharmaceutical industry's profit-generating drugs. Some 20 years ago, UCLA published a study which found that three months of intensive talk therapy could produce the same physiological changes in the brain as the use of pharmaceuticals. My naïve conclusion was that this almost poetic discovery would immediately lead to a dramatic increase in funding for the field of clinical psychology. Very naïve indeed, as it was pointed out to me that time is money; it is much more cost-effective simply to prescribe a pill. Maybe we have already arrived in the Brave New World, as envisioned by Aldous Huxley? Biology's so-called fringe researchers, who decided to look at not just the genetic make-up of the cell but to study the discarded protein layers instead, have come up with some interesting findings.

In his book *The Biology of Belief*, cellular biologist Dr. Bruce Lipton demonstrates how it is ultimately the perception of an environment that makes the protein send a signal to the gene and causes it to behave in one way or another. Therefore, the perception and reading of one's environment as a whole can be crucial to how the body acts and responds. This is murky terrain, of course. It's very understandable that the world of academia prefers the nicely ordered Descartian way of seeing the world as a fixed mechanical matter rather than a community of unpredictably behaving waves of energy.

And this brings us to even more treacherous terrain, to a field where new ideas of biology and psychology merge. It may well open the door to paying more attention to how one of the most precious organisms in the universe—the human brain—is created, developed and brought into the world. I find it staggering that this information is now so commonplace that one can watch documentaries on the subject on the National Geographic channel any given Saturday morning. Thanks to microscopic cameras implanted in the mother's womb, footage shows that the fetus is not some mindless thing, as long believed, but an actual being with a fairly developed mind. The research points out that the delivery, though significant, is a relatively minor event in the baby's overall developmental process.

While the child is growing inside, the mother's unconscious mind acts as a super computer, writing into the fetus's mind all of the survival codes passed down through hundreds of thousands of years of evolution. Nature, in its intelligence, ensures that this process takes place automatically, as computer companies do; a lot can go wrong if you start playing with these processes manually. The problem with having pre-wired DNA is that much of this software is terribly archaic and not at all useful for dealing with the intricacies and challenges of the 21st century. Here we are, born with the reflexes that would have made a lot of sense 200,000 years ago—like how to handle a wild animal with rock or spear—but with only minute evolutionary development when it comes to social intelligence, which is arguably the main ingredient for a successful life and career, no matter what field you're in.

Dr. Bernard Bail, a lone voice in the field of psychiatry, is despised by representatives of the Freudian school for taking Dr. Freud's insights and expanding upon them based on new biological findings. In his book *The Mother's Signature*, Bail quotes the findings of Harvard evolutionary biologist Dr. David Haig, who has been able to show that in pregnancy, the mother turns on or off certain genes of the fetus. "There is, he says, "an unconscious struggle" between a mother and her unborn child over the nutrients she will provide… His (Dr. Haig's) theory also explains a baffling feature of developing fetuses: the copies of some genes are shut down, depending on which parent they come from. Dr. Haig has also argued that the same evolutionary conflicts can linger on after birth and even influence the adult brain. New research has offered support to this idea as well. By understanding these hidden struggles, scientists may be able to better understand psychological disorders like depression and autism."

Bail incorporated these findings into his analytical practice, realizing that it's much more logical to presume that it is not the baby that harbors Hamlet-like fantasies of wanting to kill its father and hijack its mother, which is what, freely translated, Freud's ideas of the Pleasure Principle come down to. Bail turned this theory on its head by suggesting that these fantasies are actually gigantic projections of the adult towards the baby. He then incorporated these findings into a holistic approach to dream analysis that helps the patient develop an inner dialog with his or her own conflicted psyche and create a path out of the early-developed survival techniques that muted the authentic identity to take on what the patient perceived as the desired identity. Bail has created a network of psychoanalysts who have adopted and included his insights into their own practices. It may be depressing at first to realize that you have spent most of your life not living from your own creative center, never taking the brand-new, eight-cylinder car that was your birthright out of the garage. Better late than never, I say, having found the process of rediscovering my own authentic voice extremely enriching, liberating and rewarding.

If we are all orphans to a certain extent, we need to first mourn the fact that we are all alone. But after that process has been completed, we can transform that aloneness into boundless joy. We have permission to let go of feelings of obligation, guilt and doubt, and start the adventure of reclaiming our true mother, Mother Nature, as the direct, unfiltered source of our knowledge and creativity. Then it suddenly makes sense why we have been feeling so uncomfortable in our mind and body; it was never ours to begin with! We've walked around in some very old shoes, with the emotional motivations and reflexes of generations long gone. Now that we've awoken and found ourselves on a dusty country road outside of town, our task is to start the journey back to our own true, original mind. That process is also the journey back to a balanced and sustainable environment. And we better find it soon, before we really outstay our welcome on this planet as rather abusive and inconsiderate guests.

Although these new thinkers are currently but a small part of the academic world, there is a growing community of scientists that understands that if you don't change the very method of observation and study itself, all that peering into microscopes is much like the locked-in mind of the autistic child; its discoveries stay inside an internal world and can't be shared with or applied to life.

So why would an artist concern himself with these questions, seemingly far removed from his own territory of the studio, brushes and paint? Because the key to being a creative person is more than walking around with the mere label of artist: someone who makes funny things like sculptures, drawings or paintings. Being creative means being an original thinker, someone who is not afraid to test the world as it is perceived against the empirical or self-experienced world. That is what the stories in this book relate to—a way of thinking that doesn't accept dogma out of hand, but seeks empirical understanding of its functioning so it can respond in a creative and effective manner.

Recent data reveals that one in four executives laid off from jobs that may never revive are contemplating starting a career on their own. It is clear that carving out an independent career path is a very different process from the adaptation techniques learned in the corporate world. A friend of mine who has been an independent graphic designer and computer programmer for most of his adult life was recently hired to help create a new web division for a Fortune 500 company. He told me that the atmosphere in the cubicle world feels very much like kindergarten, and what takes a full workday to accomplish in the corporate environment takes about 10% of that time in his own practice.

The exciting thing about the time we live in now is that the creative mind is poised for recognition as the dominant and most important source of intelligence. Meanwhile, the rational side of the brain, the bookkeeper who does the calculations to see if the CEO's creative dreams can be realized, can relax and do the work it was trained to do. In the corporate world, an army of accountants hijacking the ship and demoting the CEO to assistant would ultimately lead to paranoid dictatorship and self-destruction. So it is in our own mind; the rational part of the brain is much better off being led by its creative, intuitive side. This turbulent time may well herald a new renaissance, a golden age, in which anyone who takes on his or her life and career with a creative, conscious mind, whether to make a painting or a spreadsheet, is an artist of life in their own right.

I hope that these stories, and the accompanying paintings that reflect my visual journal over the last twenty years, may inspire businessperson and artist alike to not be afraid of crossing boundaries; of using the calculator instead of the brush sometime, or the palette knife instead of the ruler. In short: a mind is a terrible thing to waste, or to leave unused. If energy is fed in equal parts to the feeling world as to the reasoning world, your mind will perform on all eight cylinders—no drugs or medication required. It is perfect as it was originally created, brand-new, patiently waiting in the garage, ready to be taken out for a spin...

BIOGRAPHY

Luc Leestemaker

BORN IN THE NETHERLANDS in 1957, Luc Leestemaker's interests in art, theater and communication led him to found an Amsterdam-based performing arts center and organize the European art collective Hart Poetry. For a number of years he headed Leestemaker & Associates, an Amsterdam consulting firm specializing in the arts, and he became the founding editor of the art/business periodical Sponsoring.

Upon moving to the U.S. in 1990, Leestemaker continued a long-standing cultural tradition in his family and committed to painting full-time, following in the footsteps of other European and Dutch artists such as Willem de Kooning and Mondrian, for whom living and working in the U.S. inspired a dramatic creative transition. His stylistic journey led from early influences by the CoBrA movement, through densely abstract expressionist compositions, to the Inner Landscape and Transfiguration series, inspired by Mark Rothko and 17th and 18th century Dutch and English landscape painters like Constable and Ruysdael. With a solid foundation of contemporary landscapes, Leestemaker's recent compositions such as Voyagers and

Map of the Wind take the viewer into a new generation of abstract expressionism, one in which landscape and abstraction increasingly merge. Recent series titled Allegories, Dreams, Songs of the Unconscious, Soliqoui, and Haiku explore even deeper layers of fluidity in his painting.

The larger canvases are first treated with a thin layer of cement mixed with raw pigment powder, then worked into with acrylic paint and finished with an oil-based varnish. This fresco technique on the canvas creates a layered, luminous sense of the work which seemingly changes in different shades of light. The smaller canvases making up the "Inner Landscapes" sets are made with the palette knife to create a rich, layered look. Landscapes have become Leestemaker's preferred subject matter, as he feels that it is in these atmospheric landscapes that he can both express his emotion/intuition of the abstract compositions as well as the universally understood language of landscape painting.

Leestemaker sees the role of the artist as shaman, or Greek priest, translating the message of the gods into humanly understood action and matter. He does not subscribe to the 19th and 20th century romantic notion that the artist must be a solitary, suffering individual who locks himself away in a state of despair, creating art that can only be understood by a select few. The tragic mistake of the romanticized artist is that he has lost half of this message. This has cast the artist in the eternal role of the outsider, whereas Leestemaker believes that the role of the artist is to fill the world with spirituality and make it whole.

Leestemaker has often found that the limitations and challenges of collaborating with a multitude of disciplines (developer, architect, designer, art consultant) become very rewarding when new solutions or ideas emerge as a result. Those solutions and challenges become part of the development and creative process reflected in his own artwork in the studio. Leestemaker's openness to collaboration has led to installations for Miramax Films; Bellagio Hotel & Casino, MGM Hotel & Casino, and the McCarran International Airport in Las Vegas; The Westin Diplomat Resort & Spa in Hollywood, Florida; the Newman Scoring Stage at 20th Century Fox; the Center for Neuroscience at Harvard University, Boston; Omni San Diego Hotel; The Beverly Hills Hotel; Banner Estrella Medical Center in Phoenix, Arizona; Genzyme, Boston; Four Seasons Resort, Bahamas; Sheraton Miyako Hotel Tokyo and Mitsubishi, Japan.

Private collectors include former President Bill Clinton and Hillary Clinton, former President George W. Bush and Laura Bush, Mrs. Nancy Reagan, Whoopi Goldberg, Drew Barrymore, Steve Carell, Esa-Pekka Salonen, David and Anne Gergen, Charlie Haden and Chris Matthews.

Leestemaker's paintings are exhibited throughout the U.S. and internationally, increasingly becoming a part of major corporate and private collections. Two retrospective museum exhibitions were held in 2004. Boston Galerie d'Orsay hosted an exhibition for the artist in 2005 with a selection of the museum works. A number of paintings were included in the 2008 Riverside Art Museum exhibition *"Plein Air Abstraction."* The documentary *"Swimming Through the Clouds"* about the artist's life and work was screened at a number of film festivals around the world and broadcast by Link TV, a culture and arts satellite network. Leestemaker collaborated with famed composer and musician Charlie Haden to create the artwork for Haden's 2005 Grammy Award-winning CD, *"Land of the Sun."* His collaboration with Hollywood's film industry has led to a number of film and television projects, including *"Spiderman," "Bringing Down the House," "Erin Brockovich," "Simone," "Shopgirl," "American Dreamz," "Spiderman III," "Fracture,"* and *"Boston Legal."*

In 2006, the award-winning Canadian composer Vincent Ho used four paintings of the artist as inspiration for a chamber music work in four parts, titled "Four Paintings By Leestemaker." Funded by the Canadian Arts Council, this work was performed at a number of music festivals throughout China. The video artist and animator Edber Mamisao choreographed a 20-minute visual interpretation of this composition, and a DVD version of this compilation is part of a comprehensive retrospective of the artist's work, published by Skylark Press.

More information about the artist can be found on his website: www.LucLeestemaker.com

INDEX

Color Plates

Page 40
Hybrid # 5
1992. 60 x 48 inches
Mixed media on Canvas
Collection Mr. G. Rose

Page 41
Untitled Landscape 2004.08
2004. 54 x 54 inches
Mixed media on Canvas

Page 42
Untitled Landscape 2008.05
2008. 41 x 33 inches
Mixed media on Canvas

Page 43
Untitled Landscape 2004.01
2004. 60 x 72 inches
Mixed media on Canvas

Page 44
Matador
1996. 60 x 50 inches
Mixed media on Canvas
*Collection Mr. & Mrs. Neil
and Sharon Hornstein*

Page 50
Transfigurations 2004.01
2004. 48 x 72 inches
Mixed media on Canvas
*Collection Mr. & Mrs. Ben
and Tracy Samek*

Page 51
Untitled Landscape 2008.08
2008. 48 x 48 inches
Mixed media on Canvas
Collection Sam S. Dahr, M.D.

Page 52
Untitled Landscape 2008.03
2008. 54 x 50 inches
Mixed media on Canvas
*Collection Mr. Doug Fisher
and Ms. Laura Ianetta*

Page 53
Untitled Landscape 2008.03
2008. 54 x 54 inches
Mixed media on Canvas

Page 54
Voyager # 10
2006. 80 x 80 inches
Mixed media on Canvas
Collection Mr. & Mrs. Scott and Carlie Kyle

Page 62
Untitled Landscape 2008.02
2008. 60 x 48 inches
Mixed media on Canvas

Page 63
Transfigurations Grande # 1
1999. 80 x 72 inches
Mixed media on Canvas
Collection Mr. & Mrs. M. Roness

Page 64
Haiku # 31
2009. 24 x 18 inches
Mixed media on Canvas
Collection Ms. Lucy Walsh

Page 65
Untitled Landscape 2008.01
2008. 72 x 60 inches
Mixed media on Canvas

Page 66
Return of the Muse
1995. 48 x 36 inches
Mixed media on Canvas
Collection Mr. C. Villani

Page 70
Inner Landscape # 35
1997. 12 x 9 inches
Mixed media on Canvas
Collection Ms. Anne Anka

Page 104
Gabriel
1995. 24 x 18 inches
Mixed media on Canvas

Page 109
Untitled Landscape # 9
2006. 72 x 80 inches
Mixed media on Canvas

Page 110
Camelot Series # 4
1993. 60 x 48 inches
Mixed media on Canvas

Page 111
Earth Songs # 1
2008. Collection of 30 canvases,
12 x 10 inches each
Acrylic on Canvas
*Collection Mr. & Mrs. Richard
and Janet Velazquez*

Page 112
Landscape 2004.02
2004. 42 x 60 inches
Mixed media on Canvas

Page 113
Blue Sky & Yellow Land
1991. 25 x 32 inches
Acrylic on Canvas

Page 114
Soliquoi # 16
2008. 48 x 48 inches
Mixed media on Canvas

Page 122
Solitary Landscape
1998. 28 x 22 inches
Mixed media on Canvas

Page 123
Birdsongs # 9
1992. 72 x 48 inches
Acrylic on Canvas

Page 124
Ode to Wagner
2004. 60 x 60 inches
Mixed media on Canvas
Collection Mr. & Mrs. Bruce and Kathy Barry

Page 125
Firebird # 2
1996. 60 x 48 inches
Mixed media on Canvas

Page 126
Untitled Landscape 2008.05
2008. 48 x 66 inches
Mixed media on Canvas
*Collection Mr. & Mrs. Tom
and Leslie Fiorentino*

Page 133
Allegories # 77
2007. 48 x 48 inches
Mixed media on Canvas
*Collection of Mr. & Mrs. Doug
and Harlene Smith*

Page 134
Voyager # 2
2006. 72 x 80 inches
Mixed media on Canvas

Page 135
Soliquoi # 37
2008. Diptych; 48 x 36 inches,
48 x 48 inches
Mixed media on Canvas

Page 136
Songs of the Unconscious
2007. 60 x 72 inches
Mixed media on Canvas

Page 137
Camelot Series # 16
1993. 48 x 60 inches
Mixed media on Canvas
*Collection Mr. & Mrs. Ben
and Tracy Samek*

Page 176
Allegories Triptych; # 78, 79, 80
2007. 35 x 23 inches each
Mixed media on Canvas

Page 181
Voyager # 38
2006. 80 x 72 inches
Mixed media on Canvas
Collection Mr. & Mrs. Kevin
and Sonia Stephens

Page 182
Voyager # 28
2006. Diptych, 80 x 96 inches
Mixed media on Canvas
Collection of Mr. & Mrs. Kiran
and Leanna Sidhu

Page 183
Voyager # 52
2006. 32 x 48 inches
Mixed media on Canvas
Collection of Mr. & Mrs. David
and Anne Gergen

Page 184
Voyager # 6
2006. 80 x 72 inches
Mixed media on Canvas

Page 185
Haiku # 6
2009. 50 x 50 inches
Mixed media on Canvas

Page 186
Inner Landscapes # 2009.03
2009. 11 x 10 inches each
Acrylic on Canvas
Collection Mr. & Mrs. Jonathan
and Nicole Bachman

Page 193
Soliquoi # 26
2009. 72 x 80 inches
Mixed media on Canvas

Page 194
Falling Water # 3
2008. 60 x 72 inches
Mixed media on Canvas

Page 195
Untitled Landscape # 7
2006. 48 x 48 inches
Mixed media on Canvas

Page 196
Soliquoi: The Road to the Castle
2009. Triptych, 80 x 72 inches each
Mixed media on Canvas

Page 209
Voyager # 1
2006. 72 x 80 inches
Mixed media on Canvas
Collection Mr. & Mrs. Ken
and Stephanie Konecoff

Page 210
Soliquoi # 38
2008. 60 x 60 inches
Mixed media on Canvas
Collection Mr. & Mrs. Mark
and Kathleen Santora

Page 211
Wanda's Dream, # 6
2008. 72 x 60 inches
Mixed media on Canvas
Collection Mr. & Mrs. Mark
and Wanda Cohen

Page 212
Untitled Landscape # 2009.03
2009. 48 x 72 inches
Mixed media on Canvas
Collection Mr. & Mrs. Peter and Julie Hill

Page 213
Untitled Landscape # 5
2006. 30 x 48 inches
Mixed media on Canvas
Private Collection